The Spirit of Wine
Finding Religion in the
Fruit of the Vine

To Life L'Chaim

*May the Spirit of
Wine be with you!*

Stephen R Lloyd-Moffett

Stephen Lloyd Moffett

For Kayou, my partner in wine and life.

Table of Contents

Introduction 1

Part I: The Spiritual Journey of Wine Devotees

Chapter 1: The Stages of Wine Devotion 9

Chapter 2: The Doctrines & Dogmas of the Church of Wine 35

Chapter 3: The Rituals of Wine 47

Chapter 4: The Mysticism of Wine 69

Chapter 5: Pinotphilia and The Religious Fanatics of the World of Wine
.... 97

Part II: Becoming a Wine Devotee

Step 1: Cultivate Connection to the Wine 111

Step 2: Mindfulness and the Art of Wine Drinking 129

Step 3: Appreciate the Mystery of Wine 141

Step 4: Create a Wine Community 161

Step 5: Discover Spiritual Inebriation 171

The Soul of Wine

by Charles Baudelaire

One eve in the bottle sang the soul of wine:
  "Man, unto thee, dear disinherited,
I sing a song of love and light divine —
Prisoned in glass beneath my seals of red.

"I know thou labourest on the hill of fire,
In sweat and pain beneath a flaming sun,
To give the life and soul my vines desire,
And I am grateful for thy labours done.

"For I find joys unnumbered when I lave
The throat of man by travail long outworn,
And his hot bosom is a sweeter grave
Of sounder sleep than my cold caves forlorn.

"Hearest thou not the echoing Sabbath sound?
The hope that whispers in my trembling breast?
Thy elbows on the table! gaze around;
Glorify me with joy and be at rest.

"To thy wife's eyes I'll bring their long-lost gleam,
I'll bring back to thy child his strength and light,
To him, life's fragile athlete I will seem
Rare oil that firms his muscles for the fight.

"I flow in man's heart as ambrosia flows;
The grain the eternal Sower casts in the sod —
From our first loves the first fair verse arose,
Flower-like aspiring to the heavens and God!"

Introduction

It is Sunday and cars file into the parking lot filled with nicely-dressed believers congregating for their regular gathering. They are greeted by a welcoming committee as officiates scramble behind the scenes to put together the final touches of the event. The bread and the wine are already arranged precisely on the table; background music sets the mood; everyone is smiling. The members come hoping to step out of their daily lives, learn something, and perhaps, find inspiration. They share a common belief in the veracity and worthiness of their cause. They come, also, to see old friends and perhaps make new ones. The building they file into, however, is not a church, but a winery. These are wine club members who have arrived to pick up their quarterly shipment. They are not traditionally religious, or perhaps they are.

This book is about those wine drinkers who are not just passionate about wine, but have a kind of religious devotion to it. If you picked up this book, it is likely that you are one of them or you at least suspect that your family members might think you are. For you, wine has, in the words of the legendary wine writer Jancis Robinson, taken "hold of a person" and sunk "its claws pretty deep." You are the wine devotees and your altar might just be wine itself. This book is here to explain the curious part of your soul that finds fulfillment at the bottom of a glass.

If you are not sure if you are a wine devotee, consider the follow quiz:

- ☐ Do you join multiple wine clubs or mailing lists, sometimes even contemplating offering everything short of your first child to get on the waiting list of wines you freely admit are cults?
- ☐ Have your vacations begun to look like wine pilgrimages, with Burgundy or Bordeaux acting as your Mecca?
- ☐ Are the folks in your tasting group some of your most meaningful relationships?
- ☐ Does your idea of a juicy scandal involve oak extract and powdered tannin?
- ☐ Do you find your blood involuntarily boil when you see someone put ice cubes in chardonnay, drink pinot from a puny glass, or mispronounce mourvèdre?
- ☐ Is your cellar the clearest sign that you must believe in an afterlife because no one could possibly empty such a cellar in a single lifetime?

If you checked a majority of the boxes above, then you just might be a wine devotee.

Perhaps you identify with the old German poet Johann Wolfgang van Goethe who responded to a question regarding which three things he would take to a deserted island if he knew he was going to be marooned there. He reportedly stated: "Poetry, a beautiful woman and enough bottles of the world's finest wines to survive this dry period!" He was then asked if he could only bring two things, which of the three would he give up? He succinctly replied: "The poetry!" The questioner was slightly surprised and pressed Goethe further: and if you could have only one thing with you, which would it be. And Goethe thought for a couple of minutes and was said to answer: "It depends on the vintage!"

If you suspect you identify with Goethe, you are not alone. Tens of thousands of people around the world would have a harder time imagining a life without wine than they would a functional Congress. Having known many of these wine devotees and have inclinations in that direction myself, I have even come to feel sorry for the spouses of wine devotees, especially the wife of the self-styled "Prince of Pinot," who once declared: "My wife says I am busy with pinot noir every waking moment. Not true, I also dream about it."

The point is that for devotees like us, wine captures our heart, mind, and soul completely. We are not just living but "living the wine life," as the author of a "wine devotional" states it. Yes, there actually are wine devotionals for those who have caught the bug. One devotional even reminds wine devotes to "set aside time and find a quiet place that is yours alone" each morning in order to "sip this book" as you journal your experiences of the "spirit" of wine leading you to *veritas*, Truth. If part of you suspects that deep truths lie hidden in opaque greenish bottles, you are on the path of finding spirituality in the fruit of the vine.

You are probably saying to yourself right now that you've never considered yourself religious or even spiritual, at least not toward wine. It is true, there is no recognized First Dionysian Church of Chardonnay, no Winemaker's Creed, and no one is dunked in a wine vat to be baptized, as appealing as that might sound to some of us if it were pinot. The argument of this book is that if you set aside the list of "official" religions in your mind and what you think *should* constitutes all the elements of a spiritual life, then you might see that wine sometime plays a similar role to other, more traditional objects of devotion such as God or the Dao. Perhaps you have had a spiritual relationship to wine all along, but you simply haven't seen it through that lens before. This book hopes to open your eyes to a potentially positive spiritual outlet by making you aware of the spiritual life you are already living. It is about making you see your relationship to wine in a new way.

As such, this book is not like other wine books: it is not a wine buying guide, a travel narrative through wine country, a primer on tasting, a textbook on wine marketing, or a technical book on winemaking. It is also not a reflection on the philosophical questions raised by wine, which has become a curiously popular genre as of late. It is not even a history of wine's relationship to religion, though it will draw upon history from time to time. It is about revealing the meaning of wine for people like us and the manifold ways in which wine can act as a replacement or surrogate for the human impulses traditionally fulfilled by organized religions. As such, it focuses on the non-physical elements of wine—the spirit of wine, if you will. It ponders what occurs when people begin to see the fruit of the vine as something sacred. The ancient world recognized it as the cult of the god Dionysius. Today, we may have all officially become wine atheists, but this book suggests that perhaps we've changed less than most people assume. It is time to found a new religion of wine.

A Taste of What is to Come

Our journey into the religious world of wine devotion has two parts. The first section is devoted to the universal fraternity of wine believers and their journey to becoming wine devotees. It provides insights into the purpose of wine rituals, wine dogmas, and the sacred world of wine. It ends with an exploration of the epitome of the wine devotees, the Pinotphiles. The second part of the books walks you through five steps in making wine spiritual in your life. Each chapter in Part II ends with some practical tips for integrating the insights of that step into your life.

Throughout the book, I will not take a stand on the most sacred of all grapes (though it is obviously pinot noir) or the most absurd forms of wine devotion (again, obviously pinot noir). I should also warn you that throughout this book, I will often glide seamlessly between talking about wine and talking about spirituality—so seamlessly, in fact, that it may be difficult to tell which one I am addressing. This style is on purpose. The facility and ease in which one can travel partially proves my point: it is sometimes mighty challenging to differentiate the two. The life of wine sometimes looks suspiciously like the religious life (and the religious life sometimes looks like the life of wine). My suggestion if you experience anxiety whether a statement is about wine or religion is to take another sip (for this book pairs well with wine) and wait to the end of the paragraph—it should be clear by then. If not, have another sip.

Part I: The Spiritual Journey of Wine Devotees

Chapter 1:
The Stages of Wine Devotion

An online community called "Wineberserkers," a sort of coven for wine devotees, has a chart that traces a spiritual progression toward wine paradise. It begins with stage one: Genesis, a wine epiphany that leads the neophyte to seek something more. Confusion follows in stage two but is resolved by becoming a disciple of a respected wine critic in stage three. Eventually an awakening occurs that leads to a quest (stage eight) that leads, almost inevitably, to Enlightenment, which is Burgundy and the discovery of its premier grape, pinot noir. However, thence you realize the cost of Enlightenment, you enter the "Dark Night of the Soul" as you come to terms that Enlightenment will bankrupt you faster than Scientology. In the final stage, you discover a cheaper paradise, Mosel, where you find your eternal rest in German riesling.

As with most satire, this reconstruction rings true, perhaps eerily so, for some readers of this book now lapping a dry riesling with a smile if not a smirk. The progression to wine heaven is probably not so linear and personally I've yet to have a Mosel that tastes like paradise but I know people who have. In fact, after studying religious people for much of my life, I find that my wine friends often look strikingly similar: both sets of friends tell dramatic stories of conversion, they attach themselves to meaningful communities, they speak like evangelists, and they sometimes veer awkwardly close to cults. This chapter explores the spiritual evolution from a wine drinker to wine devotee.

Addressing the Wine Skeptics

If, in the midst of a vulnerable moment induced by a sultry syrah, you admit in a whispered voice to your drinking companions that you might just be a wine devotee, you will likely be met with skepticism. I've discovered that such skepticism has less to do with the spiritual orientation of the drinking friend and more to do with the wine they have consumed that night. For skeptics, wine is a beverage; for devotees, it is so much more.

I learned this lesson once while making wine one day in Australia. I was shoveling grapes into a fermentation bin with a man who, a few years prior, had left his job in the city to follow his passion for wine every day. He landed as a cellar rat in a small, boutique winery in McLaren Vale. We chatted as we worked and I brought up a nearby winery I had visited previously that produced more than 10 million bottles a year. Before I could even finish my first thought on this goliath winery, he interrupted me: "That isn't a winery, it is a factory; they don't make wine, they make a beverage." I learned that moment that some wine is wine and other wine is a beverage and you shouldn't mix the two with wine devotees.

Recovering from my faux pas and reflecting upon the Yoda-esque correction, I came to see his point: some wines are little different from Coca-Cola, Heineken, or Starbucks. Their wine labels may provide a year and a place, but the goal of the mass producer of wine is consistency across years and across bottles. Just as it would sound very strange to say that Coke bottled in Atlanta has more profound flavors than Coke bottled in Los Angeles or that you preferred the 2015 vintage of Coke to the 2016 vintage, when the makers of Jacob's Creek make ten million bottles of cabernet-syrah a year, they want them all to taste the same and be consistent across the years. It takes a wine factory to reach this goal, not a winery.

Let's agree to admit that we all begin as consumers of wine beverages. A privileged few cut their wine teeth on Château Mouton-Rothchild, but the rest of us began our wine journey with our friend Chuck Shaw and our trusty drinking partner with the Yellow Tail. Most of us can remember a time when we were attracted to wines with clever critter names and cute labels. Most wine drinkers never leave that phase and thus have a hard time imagining that wine could be a vehicle of transcendence. The average price of wine purchased in the last five years in America according to the market surveyor Nielsen hovers around $6. One out of every four bottles of wine sold costs less than $3 and nine out of 10 bottles of wine sold in the U.S. cost less than $12. Depending on the study, somewhere between 75% to 90% of wines are consumed within 24 hours of buying and 95% within a week. Less than five percent of wine drinkers read any wine publications. Yet, wine devotees are part of the few who move beyond seeing wine merely as a beverage.

For wine devotees, the juice of Dionysius is not merely a means of quenching thirst or inducing drunkenness—notice that you sip a wine but drink a beverage—but vehicles of transcendence. They open new worlds to the drinkers, not just about wine but about life. Wine importer Kermit Lynch conveys this notion when he describes tasting a label-less burgundy with a friend: "The bottle shape was Burgundian and so was its magical aroma, evoking a response like the first hearing of a Bach piece, that awe that something so extraordinary can exist, something manmade."[1]

Wine devotees believe that wine has this capacity to uplift the soul and transcend ordinary existence, while wine beverage drinkers have not had any experience that suggests such potential. The ancients of the Middle East would have called it a vehicle to Gnosis, Insight. In fact, the Latin writer Horace thought that wine could do even more: "Wine brings to light the hidden secrets of the soul, gives being to our hopes, bids the coward flight, drives dull care away, and teaches new means for the accomplishment of our wishes." Contemporary wine devotees use different words but agree with the sentiment, especially when "the accomplishment of our wishes" involve finishing the bottle.

Wine, for them, has become simultaneously a revealer of the self, a portal to the infinite, and a bringer of dreams. A wine beverage never aspires to such heights. Wine for the devotee has travelled from their lips through their head and now is firmly lodged in their heart and soul, the territory of the sacred. It becomes a gateway to paradise and harbinger of hope. For devotees, wines don't just whet your appetite like a beverage but some bottles have the capacity to totally transform you.

The Beginning of a Wine Devotee: Cabernet Conversions and Riesling Repentance

When a fisherman named Andrew first saw the new preacher in town, Jesus of Nazareth, he dropped his fishing nets and followed him. When the companions of Guatama Siddhartha first heard the newly enlightened Buddha, they renounced the world and became his first disciples. A young Cassius Clay read a magazine called "Muhammad Speaks" and began his slow evolution into Muhammad Ali. Conversion tales are a staple in religious literature. They usually tell of an inner transformation that forever alters the convert's world. Moments of conversion are memorable, especially for wine devotees.

Nearly every wine devotee has a conversion story such as this one, by the Australian wine writer Campbell Mattinson:

> I liked wine before I liked beer, but I drank and enjoyed all kinds of funny, sweet, tropical wines for many years before the night when it all ramped into a kind of obsession. Truth is, wine hit me like a rainmaker and damaged me forever...it hit me like a magnum to the back of the head (whether my common sense, or the magnum, shattered is still up for contention)...it was a night when the alcohol flowed like stupidity at a football club and something

in me changed, forever, at the sip and the taste and the sensation of one particular wine. I drank it, and as I did so it was like I was being bitten by Dracula or a werewolf or, more appropriately, by a malaria-carrying mosquito. Something went funny in me. My heart got an erection. From that moment, I may have looked the same, but I was changed....I'd been a journalist, that night, for ten years, and a wine, wine *cooler* or scotch-and-cola drinker for the lot of them. But that night something switched over, turning me from a wine drinker to wine crazed. It was my fresh-oyster-plucked-and-shucked-in-a-French-bay moment. My white-truffles-in-a-Florence-trattoria revelation. I sipped, I swigged and I was hooked. It was like losing my innocence, and starting a war at once. I fell in love that night. With wine.[2]

I know this description sounds like the beginning of a Guy Noir episode, but it is really his cousin pinot noir. Nevertheless, in my research, people told me similar tales again and again, even with a straight face. They often spoke in hushed tones describing their epiphany moment, the moment when their whole life changed because of a grape encounter. These are the moments when people convert to wine. They struggle to find words to describe their experience, and truthfully, unless you've had that experience, you probably don't get it. If you do understand, it is probably because you at least flirt with being a wine devotee and can recall a similar experience in your own life.

I remember my own: a bottle of Santa Ynez's Beckmen syrah by a pond on a sunny winter afternoon with some of my new colleagues. Perhaps you can recall a particular wine that shifted your perception of wine? Wine writer Matt Kramer calls such a moment a "virginal epiphany:" "the first time the scales fell away from your palate and you saw the wine light, I'll bet you anything that you barely knew which end of bottle had the cork....Your senses open; your mind swells. Life seems richer, finer, fuller. You feel like you're in on a great secret..."[3]

These are life-changing moments—one of the few events alongside such moments as your first love, the birth of your first child, and the death of a loved one that regularly appear when you give the two minute version of your life's resume. It is the experience that after it happens makes you not sleep at night or makes you call your mother to inform her that you are moving to France for a vintage.

Most of all, with religion and wine, conversions are always beginnings for something more; they give you a taste, quite literally in the latter case, for what you want in your future life. Your world is turned upside down and you are certain of only one thing: you want more. It is impossible to have such an experience, shrug your shoulders, and move on in life as if it never happened. Not all wine or religious conversions are dramatic, but they all lead to quests, sometimes just to have a similar experience but usually to have an even greater one; after all, just imagine the experience with an even better wine, appreciated with more knowledge, and paired perfectly with the finest food? You are now a believer. People outside the family of believers don't understand it, but those outside the church rarely do either, or they would be inside it.

Joining a "Church" of Wine

Wine conversions are very personal moments for individuals, especially as they look back and realize that their life pivoted with that one glass of wine. Yet, those experiences rarely occur alone. Wine is most at home in communion, the coming together of people with the fruit of the vine at the center. Clifton Fadiman notes that "A bottle of wine begs to be shared; I have never met a miserly wine lover." Neither have I. The greatest joy of a wine devotee is sharing the best wine of their life with somebody else.

There is a Spanish saying that captures this dynamic: *El Vino, para que sepa a vino, bebelo con un amigo.* For a wine to taste like real wine, it has to be drunk with a friend. Drinking wine is then almost inevitably an inter-subjective experience: one that should happen with others. But the beauty of a great wine is that it makes a friend of the person with whom you share it. Wine breeds the communities that provide the fellowship to support one's journey into a life of wine.

My field of Religious Studies has analyzed the factors that lead a casual adherent of a religion to become a fervent devotee. For example, Jewish scholars have analyzed the factors which most contribute to Jewish children retaining their faith once they grow up. The variables included learning Hebrew, the level of religious education, having a bar/bat mitzvah, synagogue attendance, and eating kosher (kashrut) in the home. To the surprise of many, the factor that far and away was most predictive of later Judaism was eating kosher in the home. The explanation given for its importance was that eating is something one does multiple times a day and so the kids were reminded of their Jewish identity any time something entered their mouths. By contrast, the other actions were more sporadic. The lesson is that repetition builds deep and strong identities to the community and its shared object of devotion.

Historically, most religions have come to the same conclusion: humans need regular reminders of what is important or else we become distracted by the attractive neighbor across the hall, the latest episode of the most recent binge-worthy show, or any other of the plentiful distractions our society heaves upon us. In fact, most religions seem to suggest that humans safely have about a three hour attention span: in Islam and in Christian monasteries, the most devoted pray five times a day to insure you won't go much more than three waking hours without a reminder. Buddhist monasteries are similar, although with meditation rather than prayer. The religion of wine is not so persistent, at least for most. However, there is recognition that for wine to grow in meaning in one's life, one needs to be in frequent contact with a group of fellow devotees. Here is where tasting groups come in.

After one's wine conversion, many people seek out other people who have had similar transcendent experiences with wine and they join a tasting group. The tasting group regularly host events, which often have themes such as a night of Argentinian malbecs, a vertical of Stag's Leap cabernets, rieslings from around the globe, curious blends, obscure varietals, or some other manner of configuring the wine world. Regular wine tastings perform the same function as regular church or temple services: they extract you from the busyness of everyday life, remind you of your ultimate concern, and link you to others who share that concern. They often become a sort of oenological Sabbath when the worries of everyday life are set aside and life is put back into perspective. In the best wine tastings, it is unthinkable to check the stock market or deal with a difficult client during a gathering; you are present, alive, thankful. Regular wine tastings are what inspires the spiritual evolution of those who have caught the wine bug.

Wine tastings often mimic traditional religious services. Typically, everyone brings a bottle of wine that will be sacrifice for the group—that is, the point of the offering is to break it open, spill its blood, and then ritually consume it. It is no different from the ancient sacrifices in which each person brought an animal offering which was then shared with everyone or Hindu devotees who bring gifts to the altar. The offering is a reflection upon you, as we will see in the third chapter, but you want to bring something commensurate with the sacredness of the event. Bringing an Opus One to a Two Buck Chuck night reeks of ostentatiousness and boorishness.

The parallel to sacrifice is not just a metaphor if one understands the role that sacrifices played in the ancient world. People did not offer rats and roaches but things of real value to the community. It was supposed to be a true sacrifice, a giving up of something important to you. On the one hand, this act conveyed to the gods your concern for them, but on the other hand, sacrificial events were always communal events. Your gift may be offered to the gods but was in actuality consumed by your peers. Your sacrifice was a concrete act of benevolence for the benefit of the whole; it publicly communicated your regard for those who lived around you.

In fact, there are stories from the ancient period of people going bankrupt trying to demonstrate their concern for the welfare of the polis, the city. A similar dynamic is at play in bringing a bottle to a wine tasting—it is a concrete symbol of your attachment to the group. Sharing a special bottle, especially one that you can hardly afford, becomes a special mode of social communication. Sacrificing a mere critter wine sends a different message altogether. Give unto others and you would hope they give unto you.

The aesthetic design of a wine tasting is also eerily like a religious event. Often times, there are rows of wine glasses sitting on a table waiting to be filled. The table stands like an altar sparkling with crystal. The glasses' purpose is to catch the blood of the sacrifice and distribute it to the faithful. Occasionally a relic is brought out—a particular rare wine such as a Château Margaux, for instance—that is nothing short of venerated, even if it is just an empty bottle (the hollow body of a previously sacrificed wine). An aura of mystery often pervades the room.

At blind tastings, either paper bags obscure the offering or the wines have been decanted using a secret code to identify the wines later. The mystery is only matched by the anticipation: Will the judges be pleased with my gift? Will I prove myself a worthy judge of others? Will we discover a truly transcendent wine tonight?

There is often someone who hedges their bet with a preemptive confession: "I didn't have an Argentinian Malbec in my cellar and I had to go to the local wine merchant to buy one so I doubt it will be any good." They are essentially asking for forgiveness from one's peers before the service begins. Absolution is usually granted out of deference for human weakness.

What follows is usually a cross between a bible study and a worship service. Much like a bible study, the congregants sit around a table with that which is sacred in front of them. The task is to understand clearly the gift that God has set before them. If performed in the right spirit, it is perfectly appropriate to pick it apart, analyze its component parts, and challenge the text/wine. Much like biblical interpretation, however, judging a wine is as much about the heart as it is the head; it is both an analytic and intuitive process. "What varietal is this?" is followed by, "Do you like it?"

Discussion and debate are encouraged at most wine gatherings—in fact, it is a primary purpose of gathering together. The very idea of a wine tasting group or a bible study is predicated on the value of pooling one's knowledge and trying to elevate each other to a heightened appreciation. The bond within the group is also critical for the second facet of a tasting: the group does not just coolly analyze the sacred but appreciates it and indeed venerates it.

Wine tasting groups rarely have formal membership rolls but often there are informal ones. They operate like a monastic order: a supplicant indicates their interest in joining the group. The elders—usually the founders of the group— gather to consider the request. If granted, the supplicant enters the community as a novice. A period of testing and trial follows which is inevitably nerve-wracking for in every religious order there are both formal and informal codes of behavior, spoken and unspoken creeds about the definition of quality, and institutional memories to which the newbie will never have access. More than anything, the initiate does not want to ruffle feathers.

Having been the fresh face at dozens of monasteries and wine groups, I can attest that the feelings are the same: trepidation that I will say or do the wrong thing; bewilderment at why some traditions evolved in the way they did; above all, wanting to belong, wanting the novitiate period to end.

The experience of tasting wine alone is not the same, much like the experience of having sex alone is rather different from having it with another. Yes, there are parallels and, in the end, the cork is popped and the juice flows, but drinking alone is not nearly as satisfying for most. Likewise, deepening one's relationship with wine happens in the context of a community. While it may be possible to become a wine devotee on one's own, I have never seen it happen. The church of wine creates the faithful within it.

Becoming a Wine Evangelist

As some stage, the passionate believer organically moves from the pew to the pulpit. History shows that as faith takes hold, it becomes almost impossible to keep it to oneself. We want to share the good things in life with others, so in the religious evolution, people move from casual adherents to a faith to active evangelists of a cause. The world of wine is no different. As people deepen their appreciation for wine, they want to share their insights with others.

Most wine devotees eventually become wine evangelists, merrily moving through life with the aim to convert as many as possible to the gospel of the grape. Unmistakably, the goal is to create fellow converts to the faith. Of course, the choice set before a neophyte wine devotee will not be presented as a leap of faith, but rather an exercise in appropriate discernment. Nevertheless, the missionary field in the world of wine is dripping with those who want to show others the oenological light.

The high priest of wine evangelists has to be Terry Theise, wine importer and author. He speaks like a Baptist preacher, but his god is the wines of Mosel in Germany. The following panegyric to Mosel seems most at home from a pulpit (or a campaign stump, though it is sometimes hard to tell the difference):

> I think that we who love Mosel wine do so with a special tenderness. That is partly because of the wines' particular sparrow charm, but if you have ever been there you find in these wines a taproot from which you can drink from your soul's purest waters. These wines do not merely hail from a culture; they're so deeply embedded in that culture you can't tell anymore where one ends and the other begins. The cohesion is both stirring and unnerving...But Mosel wine hails from someplace true in the world, and from the people connected to it and the culture they created, which honors the connection. Can we ever have too many reminders that such places persist? If you're sinking into ennui as yet another corporate type presses his marketing strategies on you, as yet another former dermatologist or veterinarian lords his milk-and-honey

lifestyle over you and you wonder what any of it has to do with wine, with why you first fall in love with wine-I have places to show you. If you're weary of reading about grape-skin concentrates and oak chips and spinning cones and must concentrators and debt service and consultants who guarantee a certain critic's score-if you're weary of even thinking about scores-I have places to show you. If you read a passage of poetry and feel that sudden silence as the world expands and deepens, and you hear yourself wonder, *I used to have this thing in my life; where did it go?* I have places to show you. They are what I wish to capture here, because the world keeps grinding us down to the nub until we forget we are even hungry or alive. But *these places are still here.* You can go to them whenever you want. You can live the life they offer. You can remove the thorn from your paw.[4]

Amen. As with all good evangelical calls, this monologue invites us not to a new kind of belief but a new kind of existence, one made possible by the wine of Mosel. If we belly up to the altar of Mosel, we are promised a richer and more meaningful life. Salvation in a glass. Eternal hope in a vineyard. This is the kind of devotion that wine evangelists hope to share with others.

However, the evangelist stage also tends to breed dissention in both religion and wine. Once, during a posh dinner in Sydney in 1977, the brash and outspoken Aussie critic Len Evans and the upper-crust and elegant British wine writer Michael Broadbent got into a heated exchange about the quality of wine. The Australian Prime Minister was in attendance and the night was already legendary because a friend of Evan's decanted a rare 1727 German Apostelwein when he accidentally dropped it, sending the contents to the floor and leading to the quick retort, "Right, shall we open the 1728 then?"[5]

The wine of the evening, however, did not land on the floor: it was a 1929 Château Haut-Brion. Evans took a sip and declared loudly it was "the dingo's bullocks" with no potential rival. Broadbent disagreed, flatly stating it was "overblown." Writer Jon Hurley recounts what happened next: "Enraged that a poncy Pom should challenge him in his lair, Evans reached over a hairy mitt to tear out Broadbent's giblets."[6] He would have been successful if it wasn't for the girth and quick thinking of the Prime Minister sitting between them, who split them up before full fisticuffs could commence between two scions of the global wine community.

The level of vigor and venom in debates among wine evangelists is one of the most puzzling aspects of the wine world for those from the outside. How can such energy be spilled over a drink? Does anyone really get that animated over extended maceration? Some have suggested that wine attracts people for whom arguing is a sport: after all, two of the best known wine critics, Robert Parker and James Halliday, both started off their careers as lawyers. The roots of this tendency, however, may be deeper than self-selection but rather can be found in the relationship between proselytizing and psychology.

We tend to think that the vigor of proselytizing and apology (defense of positions) stems from confidence—we are sure we are right, and want to share it with the world—but the evidence suggests otherwise. Proselytizing and strident defense tends to *increase* when confidence wanes. It is like the marginal note I once saw of a fellow presenter at a conference that stated: "Weak point. Speak loudly." This dynamic seems to be the paradoxical drive behind a lot of evangelism: proselytizing and fervent defense are signs of doubt, not confidence.

The seminal study was from 1956 when a series of academics infiltrated a doomsday cult after the predictions of a cataclysmic event failed to materialize. Although this event led them to doubt, their response was to double-down: defend the non-event to mean that God spared earth because of their belief and initiate a significant campaign to proselytize others to hold their beliefs. Several later studies have shown the same result: insecurity of belief leads to more vehement and righteous voices reaching out to others.

Perhaps this dynamic helps us understand why wine arguments within wine evangelism are so legendary. Judgments about the quality of wine always have an unavoidable degree of subjectivity. Study after study reveal that even experts should not be confident in even determining white wines from red wines, let alone reliably agree on the best wines from a blind tasting. We know that factors such as price and even the music playing in the background can shape how one experiences the wine. All these factors suggest that certainty is particularly elusive in the wine world—any belief that pinot is the only great wine is grounded ultimately more in hope than anything that we can scientifically measure. As a result, perhaps those who care passionately about wine *and* yet are subject to its inherent uncertainty act like religious believers faced with doubt: they become more fervent and more public in their defense.

These arguments seem petty and unduly intense for those outside the wine life--red versus green pepper undertones or the proper tannin level—but perhaps the reason is not to be discovered in the wine tasters' personality but rather a function of the degree of uncertainty inherent in the practice of tasting wine combined with the important role wine plays in their lives. It is a new form of the famous medieval debate of how many angels can fit on the head of a pin. Likewise, wine bloggers with venom are the wine world's nun with rulers. Those loudly and publicly bemoaning the inevitable death of wine due to globalization and commodification of taste are the equivalent of those sidewalk preachers announcing, "Repent, for the End is near!" These are all stock characters in the history of religions. Evangelical and rancorous wine lovers are not just trying to impart information but steer you to their favored place in the sacred wine map. In doing so, they might just save your wine soul— and their own in the process.

Creating a Wine-Centered Life

In the third century, a pious monk from Spain named Vincent stopped by the side of the road to talk with a vintner. As they chatted, his donkey nibbled the tops of some of the nearby vines. The grower was annoyed but by the autumn harvest these vines had produced the most beautiful and bounteous fruit of the vineyard. Vincent, or more properly Vincent's donkey, had accidently discovered the art of vine pruning. Vincent returned to Valencia, but during the great persecution of 304 he refused to burn his copy of the Bible despite fierce pressure by the governor. He was imprisoned, tortured, and eventually martyred by having his body crushed. It is said that his blood sprung from his body like wine from a wine press.

It has been relayed that Vincent was rewarded with heaven for his martyrdom but the story continues: Vincent found heaven disappointing. After all he had done to earn heaven—the years of prayers, fasting, celibacy, and then his torture and martyrdom—he found that heaven lacked good wine. God, a Being of infinite compassion, gave him permission to revisit Burgundy and Bordeaux on a sort of vacation from heaven. Vincent, however, did not return from his sojourn in the vineyards. Angry, God sent angels to retrieve him, who they found him drunk in a wine cellar. God was so annoyed with Vincent, he turned him into stone that instant. He can still be seen at Mission-Haut-Brion in Bordeaux, clutching a glass of wine and a bunch of grapes. Saint Vincent, who has wine in his name (*vin* is wine in French), has become the patron saint of wine growers. Whenever there are difficult vintages in Burgundy or Bordeaux—and there are many—St. Vincent never fails to deliver, or almost never. Perhaps he wants a bit of the angels' share.[7]

Each January around the time when the first signs of new growth appear in the vineyards, the most important festival of Burgundy happens: *Saint-Vincent tournante*. The name, Touring St. Vincent, comes from the fact that it rotates among the villages of Burgundy each year. Over a hundred thousand people participate on a normal year. It begins with a grand procession of winemakers shouldering mini-sleighs bearing carved wood images of their patron saint. The procession ends with a vast church service, with a free wine tasting outside, of course. The vintners are dressed up, complete with colorful ribbons representing the necessary elements for a successful year: yellow represents sunshine, green represents the grapevine, and red represents the earth. Burgundy lovers from around the world travel to join in. The festival culminates with three grand banquets and a lot of tipsy guests. It is also an example of the way in which evangelists slowly evolve to become devotees.

As wine devotees sink deeper into devotion, they might notice that their calendars are filled less by saint days and birthdays, but by wine events. As with previous generations' religious calendars, the number and variety of these events are mind-boggling. There are events associated with particular grape varieties, regions, times of year, and particular wineries. We could follow the sacred calendar for any of these sects, but perhaps pinot is most illustrative: for the passionate Pinotphile (a redundant descriptor), the year begins down under with the Central Otago Pinot Noir Festival in January in New Zealand. Nearly every weekend thereafter, there is an event somewhere in the world dedicated to Pinot, with the highlights being the World of Pinot in March on California's Central Coast, Oregon's International Pinot Noir Celebration, and Burgundy's infamous Hospices de Beaune auction in November. The year is marked not by months named after Roman gods but by pinot events.

Over time for devotees, the identification of holy land also begins to shift. It is less Jerusalem or Mecca and more the walled vineyard of Clos do Vougeot in Burgundy or the Hill of Grace in South Australia or To Kalon in Napa. These become the pilgrimage sites of wine devotees. The Hindus use a term called *tirtha,* crossing over points, to describe their pilgrimage sites. However, they are not physical crossing-over points but a crossing over in terms of planes of existence—a crossing over between the ordinary, earthly plane to the realm of the divine or sacred. For the true devotees, the vineyards are the places where the divine world touches the human world and creates life, and that eventually finds its way into a bottle.

For wine devotees, this land becomes hallowed ground and they treat such vineyards as religious devotees have for millennia: they endure hardship to get there, they kneel, they kiss the ground, sometimes tasting it. Then, they will bring back a rock from the vineyard, a cork from a bottle from the tasting, or a photograph with the winemaker to remind them of their visit. These are the religious souvenirs that can take them back to the source whenever they want, or perhaps whenever they need. The wine evangelists now have organized their lives around those special times and places that reveal moments of oenological wonder; they are becoming mature devotees.

The Final Stage: The Lure of the Cult (Wine)

One of the greatest debates in the world of wine centers on which varietal is most noble. Many wine devotees will proclaim quite readily that cabernet is the King of Wines and the "only grape that would be tolerated in Heaven" only to find a correction from the other side of the room that

Burgundy has always been the wine of kings. In Germany, it is said that gewürztraminer, muscat, pinot gris, and riesling are all "noble" grapes, but riesling is alone the king. One winemaker told me that only syrah has a "warm heart" while all the other grapes are apparently frigid. While some wine devotees are avowed polytheists, most tend toward monotheism and focus on a single grape that they find most compelling. Their Chosen Grape is their denomination and every denomination thinks it alone holds the Truth. So the path to becoming a wine devotee, much like religion, is often in danger of veering toward dogmatism.

The most passionate religious devotees often fall into what have been traditionally called cults; wine devotees are no different. The passion fueling wine devotion often leads the extremists to seek out small producers known as cult wines. No one seems to know the origin of the term cult wine—it developed probably in the late 1980s to describe wines that are reviewed highly by important critics but that are made in such small quantities that they develop a sort of mystique around them. They are the wines you hear about but usually do not get to taste: Harlan or Screaming Eagle in the United States; Valandraud in France; Pingus in Spain, Tua Rita in Italy; Three Rivers in Australia. The few chosen ones who gain access to these rare incarnations of Pure Bliss display a sort of religious zeal toward them.

Like members of religious cults, they are irrationally fervent in their beliefs and willing to sacrifice nearly anything to be a part of the club—over $1000 a bottle is not uncommon. The Guru or Master responsible for the wine (it would be disrespectful to simply call him/her a winemaker) becomes a cross between an unusually reclusive Hollywood celebrity and an oracle of the earth. Those in the club (and it is usually literally a wine club) hang on his or her every word like a prophet. And the gatherings for these cult wines are the most exclusive events, usually late at night where the initiates come together in praise of their ideal. The wine, as the object of devotion, gains a mystique that draws even more interest, thus making it even more scarce and the value/status that much higher. When people begin to call the purchasers of the wine "followers" rather than "consumers," then it has become a cult wine.

Why are people drawn to cults, especially when the term has such pejorative and negative connotations? After all, the media is filled with sordid tales of impressionable young people seduced away from society, but eventually rescued by their loving family members and successfully deprogrammed. However, no one grows up dreaming of the day when they can call to tell their parents that they joined a religious cult. Furthermore, a cult never considers itself a cult; rather, they are living authentic lives of appropriate spiritual devotion. The term cult is what outsiders call new religions that are usually small that they find particularly distasteful.

People love to ask those of us who study religion what is the difference between a cult and a religion? The glib but common response is "one hundred years and one hundred thousand followers." The point is that there is little difference qualitatively between a cult and a religion; the difference lies in the number and fierceness of devotees and the newness of their beliefs.

In the cult heydays of the 1960s and 1970s, it was widely believed that members were victims of charismatic leaders who brainwashed their victims. This myth led to a questionable industry for deprogramming that rose and fell quickly in a tangle of lawsuits and law violations. But numerous studies have shown that people join cults primarily for the feeling of belonging that they receive. It is not surprising that many of the most notorious cults went by the name "the Family": Anne Hamilton-Byrne in Australia, Charles Manson in California, David Berg in California (formerly the Children of God), Stewart Traill of Pennsylvania's "Forever Family" movement, and Jim Jones, whom everyone called "Dad" to the "Rainbow Family" before they drank the Kool-Aid. New Religious movements give adherents a strong sense of group identity—a new family—in which they find purpose and meaning that they lacked previously.

The search for the most transcendent wine experience thus often ends with a search for belonging in a world defined by wine. When you join a cult wine club, you are a part of a wine family now with others on the allocation list. At the very least, you are "somebody" in the wine world if you can get on Harlan's mailing list; casually mentioning your case of Pingus is a social signal that you are part of the new wine elite; there are no secret handshakes in the cult of Screaming Eagle, but there are knowing nods. Exclusivist wine positions produce exclusivist people. Those who are dedicated to cult wines crave not so much a unique taste but a unique status as part of a privileged group, despite what they may report to others. The high price of membership— like Scientology, you really have to pay to play in this world—

just validates its importance. The outside world might think them mad—but the devotees of cult wines live for drinking the Kool-Aid.

One of the most distinctive attributes of human experience is the spiritual element of existence. Pigs don't pray; ants have no sense of an afterlife; monkeys can't meditate. Yet, some of the earliest marks of civilization were religious in character: images of goddesses scratched onto cave walls and burial sites that include signs of a belief in the afterlife. Some of the most enduring artistic and literary expressions across time have been inspired by the deep-felt spiritual connection to something greater. Nearly all indigenous populations thrive in the spiritual realms; the only hardcore materialists we find are in the modern, western world. Humans, it seems, are *homo religiosos.*

As a scholar of religion who teaches in a wine region, I have to admit that I didn't initially recognize the spiritual roles that wine was already playing in people's lives. Nevertheless, as I became more involved in the world of wine, the connection to religion seemed inescapable: people told me conversion stories, their wine groups came to look like churches, some began to sound like dogmatic evangelists, and more than a few seemed to be lured by cult wines. In short, they acted the part of traditional fervent devotees. Some people will be troubled by the suggestion that wine can be a spiritual vehicle and act as a sort of surrogate for religion. Yet maybe their view of God is just too small, which is strange considering that many of these people already believe that God can be found in bread and a communion cup. Maybe we simply need to shift our expectations for the spiritual journey and no longer limit the paths to those traditional religions found in surveys. After teaching religion for many years, I have come to hold that there are many paths to divinity, and wine is one of them.

Chapter 2:
The Doctrines and Dogmas of the Church of Wine

The First Church of Wine (membership unknown) is one of numerous groups who have put together versions of the Ten Commandments of Wine. Among their commandments are: Thou shalt have no beverages before me; Thou shalt not covet thy neighbor's wine; Thou shalt not bear false witness against any vineyard; Thou shalt not serve wine in an improper vessel; and Thou shalt not drinketh white zinfandel.[1] The commandments are in jest, I think, but they speak to a tendency in religion and wine: the development of codes of right and wrong that are communicated to all new initiates and expected of the faithful.

These wine dogmas are presented as truths about the world that those who believe in wine must embrace: the 2005 Bordeaux vintage is objectively superior to the 2004; red wine overpowers all but the smelliest of fish; wine varietals each require its own special glass for proper appreciation; zinfandel is incapable of producing age-worthy wines; non-vintage wines are all plonk; all good wines need cork stoppers to age properly; never drink wine from a can; and the list could go on.

These truths comprise the knowledge base that can be employed to sort out true devotees from the mere amateurs. Perhaps you've heard a question like the following: "Would this California Meritage be more similar to the Right Bank or the Left Bank, do you think?" The questioner really is not seeking information, but rather fishing for a sign that one knows the codes and commandments. A correct answer conveys that you are part of the Church of Wine. It is the secret handshake of the wine fraternity.

It is also precisely why only some people laugh when Basil Fawlty says in *Fawlty Towers*, "I can certainly see that you know your wine. Most of the guests who stay here wouldn't know the difference between Bordeaux and Claret!"

These wine dogmas are presented to new devotees as so natural that other options are literally unfathomable. For example, few people in the world of wine give a second thought to the natural synergy between oak and wine. We assume that, generally speaking, wine simply tastes better after maturing in oak; after all, most of the highest priced wines in the world see extended periods in new oak. However, using oak was a distinctively French innovation whose current near-ubiquity says more about the deep imprint of France on the wine world than any inherent advantage. The signature of the Greeks was to add pine resin and various pitches to their fine wine; the Roman writer Pliny compares the flavors imparted by them like wine writers today speak of different oak.[2] The Romans assumed that fine wine included the adding of fresh spices such as cloves, cardamom, cinnamon, saffron, and ginger. Today, retsina in Greece and Glögg in Nordic countries carry on these respective traditions and these could have been the norm if history had turned in a different direction. In Napa, however, one would be run out of the valley for even suggesting adding either spice or pine tar to cabernet.

In fact, even the choice of oak rather than some other wood is also largely accidental: historically some wines were aged in chestnut, cherry, or redwood barrels; balsamic vinegar today in Italy is still aged in a variety of different woods, each imparting its own unique character. There is no reason why we could not have blends of wines aged in different woods.

Perhaps the most foundational dogma in wine is limiting it to grapes. Theoretically, nearly any fruit or berry with enough sugar content can be fermented alongside wine. We could one day have a market for cherry-blueberry-merlot wine or Mangosteen-rice-cabernet wine. However, wine devotees are dogmatically purists: no inter-species fraternization is appropriate or at least one should respect the 'natural' agricultural segregation of wine grapes from other fruits.

Within the dominant wine creed, blending one grape varietal with another is acceptable, except not for pinot Noir, whose line must be kept eugenically pure. Can you imagine even a pinot noir- gamay blend? A few heretics dare to buck the rules, but they are often ostracized to the "other" shelf in the wine store. Likewise, with few notable exceptions (such as the Super Tuscan), varietal borders are largely respected. A mutt wine like a pinotage - nebbiolo- touriga nacional blend strikes most of us as decidedly unorthodox in the wine world. However, a 50-50 blend of cabernet and riesling would be sacrilege! It seems the wine world strongly affirms oenological segregation between red and white grapes. A little blending of white wine in red wine is accepted but as long as it is not too noticeable, especially in Australia where not following rules is central to their origin and heritage.

These 'rules' for the wine world could be multiplied but at this point, we should stop and recognize that the reaction that most of us wine devotees are showing right now reveals that we are far more dogmatic than we like to think. And the secret to the power of these doctrines is that we think they are just the way the world works, instead of the choices of our wine forefathers and mothers.

The durable character of these wine dogmas is due in part because the central aspect of wine culture—taste—is an area that lies beyond science. The taste of wine may have a biological component—scientists can point to where bitterness is experienced on the tongue, for example—but there is no objective and verifiable mechanism to judge the quality of a wine. A scientist can show you that if I drop an anvil from a building, it will fall every time because the existence of gravity is a scientific law; by contrast, I can offer the same bottle of wine—even a famously good wine such as a 1947 Chateau Cheval Blanc—to ten different lucky people randomly selected and they will not all agree on how it tastes, let alone whether it is good. We may be able to one day invent a machine that could scientifically isolate certain flavor compounds within a wine but it will not judge whether a wine is beautiful or move a drinker to tears.

The Spirit of Wine

Here is where wine begins to look and act like a religion needing dogmas: at their core, both wine and religion deal in areas that are largely *unverifiable* and *subjective*. Religion deals in the unseen and future worlds. The great debates of religion—the existence of unseen beings such as gods and demons, the security of an afterlife or reincarnation, the source behind apparent miracles, concepts of divine justice and judgment—these are debated with such ferocity precisely because they are so difficult to prove in terms that are acceptable to most if not all; despite centuries of trying, no one has proven the existence of God in a way that most people find convincing. Likewise, someone who has experienced God directly has almost no chance of conveying that experience to someone who has no sense of transcendence.

Wine, like religion, is a squishy field where universally accepted metrics of evaluation are scarce and subjective experiences are hard to convey. Even the most scientific-oriented wine taster has trouble proving whether a wine with a faint whiff of barnyard is a fault or shows character, or why good wine does not add spices but may add tannin and tartaric acid or why fish should be served with a dry white wine. Although wine writers will try, the great wines lie just beyond description and even the most eloquent of wine writer cannot convey their most elevated wine experience to someone whose primary experience of wine comes from a box. The unverifiable and subjective nature of both wine and religion make them both particularly malleable to social and political forces to influence the orthodox dogmas that direct people.

The Aroma Wheel

An example of this process can be found in the story of a tool that has become ubiquitous in most wine tasting classes, the aroma wheel. The aroma wheel was invented by a food scientist from UC Davis department of Enology named Ann Noble. Her desire what to create an "objective" framework for wine description. It was a well-intentioned attempt to put some structure and order into wine tasting and virtually every wine educator, particularly in the new world, has used it since its arrival on the scene in 1980s. The wine students at my university carry them around like seminarians carry bibles. It is a staple of all the "Wine for Dummies" courses offered at wine shops.

The wheel is divided into three tiers: the widest is comprised of broad categories such as fruity, vegetative, nutty, etc.... Each of the next two layers gets more specific, such as the tropical fruit section dividing into pineapple, melon, and banana. The idea is that it is supposed to act as a sort of tuning fork for your nose: it allows you to identify the aromas that are coming out of the wine.

For many new wine enthusiasts, it has become a crutch: one tastes a wine and then spins the wheel looking for anything that vaguely resembles what you smell. Its widespread use has resulted in precisely its original intent: a standardized way of conceptualizing our experience with wine. Neophyte wine tasters train their palates with the wheel and these palates in turn train other ones so that the aroma wheel establishes orthodoxy for wine tasting. At least in the new world, an instructor in the sensory evaluation of wine that does not use it is instantly branded a dangerous heretic, like a Christian theology professor who eschews the Bible.

As a tool of thought regulation, the aroma wheel operates much like a catechism does for religions. The power of the catechism is not just that it gives the answers but it defines the questions for us; catechisms lay out for us the important questions in life and then provide the orthodox, approved responses. The aroma wheel does the same: it leads us to ask certain kinds of questions: what fruits or nuts do I sense, rather than other questions, such as what feelings, mental images, or memories does a wine evoke? It then supplies a multiple choice answer box to choose the 'right' answer, which is usually confirmed by a wine expert trained directly or indirectly at one of the seminaries.

It alleviates or at least lessons the anxiety associated with tasting but it limits the experience of wine to narrow preset categories of physical descriptors to which our nose is directed.[3] For example, the tropical fruit section has just pineapple, melon, and banana as choices, forgetting some of the most interesting one such as guava, mango, or papaya. It is not that one is forbidden to recognize these aromas (just as religions cannot forbid any heretical thoughts from popping in one's head), but the social pressure results in a narrowing of the search that results in aromatic blinders being set up.

I noticed this once when, to the consternation of his mother, I would give small sips to my son during his early years and asked him to describe the wine: untouched by an orthodox wine education, he would sometimes come up with creative descriptors ("strawberry poprocks after drinking orange juice" for a light pinot) that would perfectly capture the experience of the wine. No wheel is big enough to put all possible physical flavors, especially in a seven year old's imagination.

The danger of the aroma wheel is not just that it is not big enough, however. Limiting descriptors to physical compounds also narrows the interpretive scope; some of the most famous wine descriptions are precisely those that are not limited to a set number of physical elements but use all of human experience to capture the wine perfectly. Although many examples could be sited, this one by Andrew Jefford about the wines of Didier Dagueneau hits the mark:

> His wines smelled not of sauvignon blanc, nor of gooseberries or asparagus or of micturating felines, but…of spring. Sipping the Buisson Renard was like standing beneath a waterfall: the flavours were clean, limpid, eerily palpable, a soft shock. The Silex was not the parody flintlock of popular myth; it was pure, sappy, soaring rich, finishing with just a hint of stone after rain. I had not been expecting this calm and majestic retreat from the varietal. I learned something new.[4]

Jefford here is a poet conveying the experience of tasting the wine rather than a scientist breaking down its chemical structure into its component parts.

When Clive Coates commented on a particular Burgundy that it "tastes like a gentleman who lost his temper for the first time" or Francis Percival praised a description of an unexpectedly big wine as "a wine for fighting," they have strayed wildly from the aroma wheel but might better convey the experience of tasting the wine than if they stuck to it. Limiting oneself to physical compounds may ultimately limit the ability to share the experience of a wine with others.

We should not even assume that prose is the best method for capturing the flavor of wine; perhaps the symbolic language of poetry is more appropriate for wine experiences; haiku tasting notes may capture a wine better than a list of aroma wheel characteristics.[5] More fundamentally, why should we stop at words? A growing chorus of voices (if you excuse the pun) has suggested that music is better suited to the experience of wine.[6] Don Blackburn of Bernardus winery in California has tested whether tasters would be consistent in linking three wines—a nouveau Beaujolais, a Californian pinot, and a Californian cabernet—with three pieces of music: Haydn's 60[th]Symphony, Mozart's 17th Divertimento, and Beethoven's 9th Symphony. He found an 85% correlation rate, much higher than with tasting notes.

It is one thing to match wine to existing music but quite another to create music appropriate to the experience of wine. An Argentinian study asked a number of different musicians to compose music to correspond to their experience of different tastes: sour, sweet, salty, and bitter. They did so with remarkable consistency and more interestingly, non-musicians could easily match the taste to the music.[7]

Similar experiments are happening within the wine world. Australian winemaker James Erskine and wine writer Max Allen have taken it one step further by composing musical pieces that go best with wine—a sort of musical tasting note. They claim a similar high level of correlation compared to written tasting notes. Technically, this process is called synesthesia, in which people experience one type of sensation with a different sense (it is said Duke Ellington saw musical notes as colors, for example).[8] While these finding are not yet scientifically verified, they point to the fact that perhaps music is a more appropriate vehicle for describing taste than words.

Freed from the orthodox trappings, other mediums might also be explored: why not create an abstract painting as a tasting note or an interpretative dance? (Stuffy wine tastings would be much more interesting!) The point is that the influence of the aroma-wheel orthodoxy is so powerful that alternative modes of wine experience are not considered; it is assumed that the descriptors on the aroma wheel reflect reality, rather than create it.

Whether it is a useful tool for describing wine or not, the political backdrop behind its place in the wine world is hidden from nearly everyone but is unmasked when one considers the story of the German version of the aroma wheel. One section of the original aroma wheel is dedicated to "chemical" properties, including petroleum, that are most often associated with either faulty wines or mature, well-made rieslings. Riesling happens to be the signature grape of Germany. However, because the chemical section of the wheel is also associated with faulty wines, the German Wine Institute decided to eliminate that section in their version altogether. Tasters trained with the German wheel must choose another area to describe their beloved riesling, a place in the wheel presumably far away from the faults section. The wheel, as with all acts of taxonomy, becomes a hegemonic tool that covertly shapes public opinion in favor of the ones who have the power to define it. A rosary cannot make people pray but its form can shape the way in which people do. The Vatican wouldn't have it any other way and neither would those who shape wine orthodoxies.

Chapter 3:
The Rituals of Wine

Sparky Marquis, the proprietor of McLaren Vale's Mollydooker winery, always greets newcomers with a wide smile while extending his left hand for a shake; he is that kind of guy. The winery name is appropriate for "Mollydooker" is slang for left-handed in Australia and he wants to invert most wine conventions. He measures his wines not with any typical metrics but something called "fruit-weight": the "velvet glove sensation of fruit that sits on your tongue before the structure of the wine is exposed," which he claims is measurable to the tenth place and is now a trademarked term. His wines have a bit of a cult following and are found in some of the nicest restaurants in the world, but they all come with instructions: after you unscrew the cap (yes, corks were so 20th century), the sommelier should pour out a bit of the wine, turn the bottle over, and shake vigorously for about a minute before serving it. Try that in

Burgundy and watch the traditional vignerons keel over one by one from heart attacks. But for Sparky, a former Amway salesman who is part showman, part mad prophet, it is all about upending the ritual world of wine.

The world of wine is soaked in rituals and traditions: bringing wine to the host of a dinner party; using a cork-screw to open the wine; toasting before the first drink; drinking champagne out of flutes; and the list could go on. Some wine rituals are regional: in China, after the obligatory clinking the glasses that follows a toast, it is rude not to drain your entire glass, flipping it over to prove to your host that you respect rises to the level of guzzling wine. In parts of Ukraine, there is a New Year's Eve tradition of inscribing your wishes for the coming year, burning the paper, and placing the ashes in your champagne flute to consume for good luck. In Japan, to celebrate Beajolais Noveau Day (when Burgundy releases their new gamay wines), there is a ritual bath in…Beaujolais Noveau. The participants are literally soaked in wine.

In fine restaurants—the lair of the sommelier—wine rituals have more pomp and circumstance than a debutante ball: the bottle must be presented label toward the host; the cork will be presented with due seriousness; the wine will be poured into particular glasses in a particular order to a particular level. Wine must be the most ritually laden drink in the world. There are so many rituals in the world of wine that we don't even notice them or reflect upon why they are there.

Rituals are nothing new to wine. The Greeks had a whole series of wine rituals that governed their symposia (literally, 'drinking together' events). The symposium proper would begin only after the food had been finished. It commences with the pouring of three libations: one to the gods, one to fallen heroes (particularly within your family) and finally one to the king of Gods, Zeus. A garland of flowers or vine leaves would be handed out to be draped around the participants necks, perfumes would be passed out, and only then could the drinking commence. The wine would always be diluted with water (or sometimes snow if it was hot out) and placed in specially-designed bowls. Drinking wine without water was seen as barbaric by the ancient Greeks. Only Dionysius himself could drink unmixed wine without a risk; mere mortals might get violent or go mad from drinking unmixed wine. They would also play a game that involved launching the dregs left within a cup and trying to land them on a disk that was placed in the center of the room. It apparently made a loud noise that they thought was riotously funny. Who said wine is for snobs?

Why do rituals emerge?

Scholars of religion have long sought to understand the purpose of rituals. In the 19th century, researchers thought that rituals emerged because they served some practical function, usually that the participants themselves were not aware of. For example, Jews and Muslims are forbidden to eat pig products because in the ancient world, pork was susceptible to transferring trichinosis, thus the *real* reason behind the prohibition on pork were health concerns. Alternatively, another scholar argues that pigs, unlike goats, sheep, and cattle, need large amounts of grain and water, which would provide competition to humans in the desert Middle East. The point is that early on, scholars assumed that there were hidden practical concerns behind these seemingly arbitrary and empty rituals.

The world of wine loves the practical arguments as much as early scholars of religion: why do we clink glasses? Because in the ancient times, there was a fear of poison so that when you vigorously clanged your glass onto another, part of the wine would spill into the other glass, thus assuring you weren't being poisoned. Why is there a punt (a convex indentation) at the bottom of wine bottles? The *real* reason is that when bottles were hand-blown, they needed a place to hold onto. Why do you hold the wine glass by the stem or base, rather than wrapping your hand around the bowl? The *real* reason is that your body warmth could affect the taste and quality of the wine. Sometimes it seems like there is someone somewhere with a theory about nearly everything in wine. Usually, these claim to have supposedly scientific or quasi-scientific bases.

Religious Studies scholars' perspectives on rituals has evolved since the 19th century. Rituals are now conceived as part of the social process by which humans navigate life with each other. They are the tools by which we communicate with each other, navigate awkward moments, find refuge from unpleasant present realities, and build the cohesiveness which forms the basis of community. This chapter brings the study of wine rituals into the 21st century by exploring some of the social roles for rituals.

Sharing Oneself through a Bottle of Wine

Three thousand years ago in the Near East, a king makes a call to a nearby ruler. He comes bearing a special wine-drinking vessel and his favorite amphora of wine, probably from a remote wine-growing region and perhaps a special vintage. Before they begin to talk, he presents the gifts to his host in a ceremony that may have been happening since the Neolithic period.[1] Comparably later in the 10th century BCE, the great King David's father Jesse sends his son to Israel's first King Saul; he offers his host a gift of a skin of wine. [2] It seems like bringing wine to your hosts is as old as hosting itself.

For most people, bringing a wine to someone's house is merely an age-old social custom that shows gratitude toward the hosts, who are opening their house to guests. Undoubtedly, it is a kind gesture, but sociologists of religion will add that it is also a mechanism for social communication. The wine one chooses sends a message about how you see the host and also the particular event. The following fictional recreation of a conversation I overheard reveals this idea:

"We're late, jump in the car! Wait, you can't bring that wine!"
"Really, why not?"
"You'll insult them—they are not white zinfandel type of people and anyway, they are serving steak; we will come across as uncultured."
"But they said it's supposed to be a casual, summertime barbeque—white zin is a picnic wine; if we bring one of the reserve cabernets from our Napa trip we'll look pompous."
"You're right. How about we bring an Australian shiraz, the one with the cute label? It tells them we are considerate enough that we thought about what they are serving but they know it costs less than $10 so we won't look like wine snobs."

"That's the problem: they know it costs less than $10. It will tell them we don't value their friendship. How about the South African wine 'Goats do Roam'—it's good, somewhat exotic but not too exotic, and it reveals we know something about wine but not too much. We can have a good laugh."
"Only wine snobs like yourself catch the allusion to Cote du Rhône, dear, but anyway we only have it in our wine rack because they brought it to our house last time."
"Good point. How about that Bulgarian red wine that we were given last Christmas by your cousin—she knows her wine, it might be good and nobody knows anything about Bulgarian wine—we can just nod with confidence as people offer their opinions. "
"Perfect, but put it in a glittery wine bag—it will make it look fancy, but not too fancy. Ugh, now we are really late."

While the details differ, this discussion has been carried out in innumerable front halls across the wine-drinking world. It reveals a conscious awareness of the degree to which the ritual of bringing wine to a host conveys social meaning. People realize that the wine they bring says something about them and, frankly, it generally makes them nervous as hell. The gift of wine is a non-verbal communication tool of tremendous power; it is a coded message in a bottle.

Of course, we have all sorts of coded messages in our lives: the clothes we wear, the cars we drive, the music we listen to, the art we appreciate, and many, many other things convey to others who we are. Yet, the ritual of bringing wine to a dinner party is a particularly highly-charged one and inevitably sends a message—even if someone brings a generic, nondescript wine, the deliberate attempt not to send a message in the end becomes part of the message. Where this ritual is firmly implanted, communicating through this ritual is unavoidable—the question is what one communicates.

For this communication system to function, however, there must be a set of symbolic meanings associated with wine that is shared by everyone involved in the social transaction. In other words, if the guest thinks that bringing pink sparkling wine is a sign of sophistication while the host can only imagine such a wine in a Barbie dreamland, the act of social communication breaks down (and doesn't spell well for the evening, either, unless it is drunk very quickly). In the scenario above, the conniving guests use this fact to their advantage by bringing an unknown wine that cannot be fit into the shared lexicon of vinological worth. Decoding these messages has little to do with the taste of the wine for the message has been delivered and interpreted before the cork is even pulled. Wine here is purely a symbol, a message *on* a bottle.

Perhaps acknowledging this role explains the unique importance of labels for wine. There is no other product for which packaging is more important, save perhaps something like bottled water where the product is essentially the same and the package is the only means of differentiation. I have never seen someone choose their beer by the label or their toothpaste by the clever design on the tube or their shoes by the box; however, wine is regularly chosen predominantly by the label. What product has its labels feature original art by Andy Warhol, Joan Miro, Pablo Picasso, and Salvador Dali as is the case with Château Mouton-Rothschild in Bordeaux?

Even when it is not world-famous artists, the label plays an unusually prominent role for wine. The reason may be because they represent attempts to "code" a social message that can be transmitted to others through the ritual of the host gift—of course, the varietal, year, price, producer, and a myriad of other factors shape the overall message, but the label is most conspicuous. Like clothes, it makes a fashion statement that is visually apparent to anyone. The best labels are the ones who perform that task most clearly. A regal label on a cabernet sends a clear message while a whimsical logo on a sparkling syrah sends quite clearly another.

Meaning in labels has been part of the charm of identifying wines ever since the inception of labels in the 17th century, when some were even made out of enamel and silver to differentiate the highest quality of wine. By the 18th century labels were full of "neoclassical design, urns, vases, cartouches, swags, and festoons."[3] In fact, the efficacy of the ritual is often determined by the transparency of the label message, especially when the receiver is only on the fringes of the wine world. If a cartoon appeared on an expensive Napa cabernet, the symbols would be crossed and my guess is that "Tweety Bird Cabernet" will never find a home on the shelf. Rather, the label must be commensurate with its overall message for the social ritual to function as it was designed. As one of the most respected British wine merchants commented about the importance of labels, "We don't sell wine, we sell luxury."[4]

The importance of wine as a symbol in this ritual is heightened for those for whom wine is a significant part of their identity. The spouses of many wine devotees have responded to wine 9-1-1 calls from prospective guests who don't know what wine to offer a host who no longer speaks the standard wine language. It is akin to being asked to offer a prayer in front of a priest or showing your self-designed doghouse to Frank Lloyd Wright.

However, the ritual of gifting wine has the opportunity to bring even more meaning for those who care deeply about it. Standing in front of a wine rack or even better, a personal cellar, is like a catalog of potential messages of varying degrees of self-revelation. Some of the bottles are coded with personal memories (this is the bottle we bought in Willamette Valley on our honeymoon) that could be shared; other bottles may be cult or iconic wines, presenting some external validation of a message; still other wines might bottle certain emotions, such as love, bravery, or a certain *esprit de vie; a* wine that you had a part in making yourself holds special potential for self-revealing.

The point is that the more sophisticated a wine devotee you are and the larger the collection in front of you, the subtler and more nuanced the message can be. The simple act of giving a bottle to a host suddenly becomes a cross between a complex social science and an attempt at expressive art. It makes you wonder what kind of wine Jackson Pollock might bring.

In such an environment, the wine you choose becomes a symbol for you as a person. Some people say that dog owners often look and act like their dogs: show me the dog and I will know the owner. Perhaps the same can be said of one's wine: a catalog of the most beloved wines of a person is a window into their soul. If you collect mostly big, bold wines, it is unlikely that you are a shy, introverted person; if you search out wines that are out of fashion, you probably imagine yourself an independent thinker who dwells outside the box; if your cellar is full of cult wines and prestige bottles, you probably concern yourself with status more than most; if you serve mostly local, biodynamic wines then it reveals your environmental stance. While the messages differ, the lesson about wine is the same: in ritual, wine becomes a symbolic mode of self-revelation. It is a weapon against isolation and a tool for forging bonds with another. There is a proverb in Bordeaux that says, "In water one sees one's own face, but in wine one beholds the heart of another." Perhaps. But first that heart needs to be revealed.

Navigating Life through Wine Rituals

Awkward moments abound in life. Sometimes awkward moments last for years, such as the teenage years. Other times, awkward moments last for minutes, such as being stuck on an elevator with just one other person for forty floors. Still other awkward moments last for mere seconds but feel like centuries, such as waiting for someone to respond to your first profession of love. One of the roles of rituals is to help us navigate these awkward moments of our existence.

The Dutch anthropologist Arnold Van Gennep argued that rituals often act as tools of transition and rites of passage; they help us navigate the movement from one mode of existence to another. For Van Gennep, rituals acted like doorways in society's house that allowed for successful transitions as one navigates life. So a bar mitzvah eases the transition from awkward preteen years to full-fledged Jewish adult. Viewing the body at a funeral is a rite that helps navigate the transition from life to death of a loved one. Flashing the lights in the foyer at a theater is a ritual that marks the transition between intermission and the play.

While the transitional process always has stages, Van Gennep called the critical phase the "liminal" stage. Liminality is a period "betwixt and between" where one is neither in the previous state nor in the future state. It is a "time outside of time" that is often marked by a radical rearrangement of social customs, a sense of mystery and emotional nakedness, as well as the breakdown of hierarchy and law. Like the Twilight Zone, normal rules do not apply but everyone accepts it because the liminal period eliminates the awkwardness and begins the process of refashioning a new reality.

In the world of wine, perhaps the customary offering of a toast before a group has their first sip of wine acts as a sort of liminal moment. After bringing wine to hosts, toasts are probably the best known and most ancient wine-related ritual. Homer in the Odyssey tells us how Ulysses drank to the health of Achilles. The term itself comes from the Latin "tostus" meaning parched or roasted and is believed to be derived from the Greek and Roman practice of putting a piece of burnt toast in a cup of wine to lessen the effects of too much acid or other off features. However, its tie to this dubious origin has been lost long ago; its persistence across millennia has more to do with the liminality it creates than its relation to wine, which is apparent when one notices when toasts occur.

The beginnings of dinner parties or celebrations are often awkward. People arrive at different times, minds are often still occupied with other items, perhaps coats or shoes are being put away or the hosts are still setting up. The ritual of offering a bottle of wine to the host only amplifies the awkwardness, for few houses are equipped with a designated place to put wine—the equivalent of a rack for coats or a counter for food; as a result, the opening of wine often takes place in an awkward place, hidden from view. The topics of discussion of these first moments are almost always surface-level small-talk: the traffic, the weather, the news of the day.

An evening begins when the wine is poured and a toast is given. It is the social cue for when a gathering of friends morphs into fellowship. It acts as a key to shift and reframes the evening. The tenor and topics of conversation will shift after the toast, even if the toast is something simple or customary. The toast is the in-between time, the liminal moment that serves as a bridge between two phases in the evolution of the get-together.

This role is most apparent when the toast commemorates a meaningful event. The toast in this case acts as an accepted forum for saying all the things that might be too sappy to say in the normal course of conversation. At other times, it is somewhat strange to gather the room's attention to profess your love for someone or your pride in someone, but it is almost expected in a toast. A sentimental story might be greeted with shifting eyes and uncomfortable cringes in another context but placed within a toast, the reaction shifts to approving nods and sweet sighs. At times, the gesture can be dramatic: it is said that there was a custom in the 18th century of men toasting a potential love interest by stabbing themselves in the arm, mixing the blood with wine, and then consuming it for her. Of course, a toast need not be sappy or dramatic to function as a period of liminality: a humorous toast filled with jokes transitions the evening into frivolity and fun. The point, however, is the same: it is a regulated signal that the period of social instability or awkwardness is over.

People historically have taken toasts quite seriously, perhaps because they are aware of the German belief that if you don't look the person in the eye while you toast, then you are penalized by seven years of bad sex. Regardless of this perceived threat, the social signals around the toast are so strong that at the extreme, the lexical meaning of the words themselves are rendered unimportant. An illustration from a colleague proves this point: he was in Europe around a table with people from numerous different countries. They poured the wine and in turn each gave a toast from their own country. "La Chaim!" said the Israeli. "Prost!" said the German. "Kippis!" said the Finn and so on. After each toast, the group repeated it in unison, lifted their glass, and clinked them together. There were two Americans in the group and when the time came for their toast, they raised their glasses and proclaimed loudly, "Lawnmower!" To which the crowd enthusiastically responded with "Lawnmower!" Clink! The night had begun.

The ritual of a toast also has a symbolic close—its own Amen. First, glasses will be lifted, literally up toward the heavens. This act serves as an offering or dedication of what is going to transpire. It is precisely the same action that a Catholic or Orthodox Christian priest takes with the chalice holding the blood of Christ just prior to communion. It is a symbolic act of dedication of what just transpired. A trumpeting of sacred touch. In the world of wine, it is the public recognition of the shift to a new phase in the evening. Much like a church, it is usually done while standing.

The lifting of glasses is followed by the clink. It is said that this tradition began in the middle ages because the sound of the glass clinking sounded like a church bell, which scared off the devil. And it does, or so my informants in the spirit world tell me. But its affinities for a church bell are appropriate: the sound of church bells is another social symbol that marks the beginning of sacred time. It tells the village that secular time will cease, if only for an hour and if only within the walls of the church. In the wine world, the clink operates in the same way: it becomes a social symbol that the liminal period that drew us away from secular time has now ceased and we are ready to begin the serious discussions. Perhaps it is why it feels so awkward to miss touching glasses with someone at the table—the period of liminality is left uncomfortably open. The cycle is incomplete; awkwardness appropriately remains.

The first recorded instance of a toast in the English speaking land comes from the fifth century and it fits this suggestion of toasts marking a shift in time.[5] The medieval historian Geofrey of Monmouth recounts an encounter between two unlikely allies: the British King Vortigern and the Saxon Hengist. The meeting was tense and the British King had every right to be worried as Hengist would later go on to massacre the Britons at the signing of a peace accord. But that wasn't known the night they celebrated the opening of a

Saxon castle and the arrival of reinforcements. It is said that the awkwardness of that night was broken when Hengist's beautiful daughter Rowena held up a large goblet filled with wine and raised it before the British King to offer the first English toast: "Lord King: To Your Health!" The gesture dispelled all awkwardness so successfully that soon the drunk Vortigern kissed her and offered anything in the world for her hand in marriage. The Saxons won the entire province of Kent, thus beginning the Saxon foothold in Briton. Today, few hope for such spoils from a toast—for most, a kiss is enough—but it was not the last time a toast changed the course of an evening.

The **Real** World, though Wine

Teaching on the coast of California means I have a lot of students who surf and a lot of surfers who are occasionally students. Boardshorts and t-shirts are the school uniform of the latter. One day I saw a favorite student who belonged to this club wearing a finely-tailored three-piece suit. I joked with him that it must be an interview day. He asked if we could talk privately. In my office, he revealed that his life was falling apart on nearly every front: his girlfriend left him, he found out his parents were divorcing, his schoolwork was not going as well, etc… As we talked through his issues, I finally asked him what was behind the dapper suit. He replied, "Sometimes when my life is chaotic on the inside, I like to look good on the outside. It sort of puts my world back together again." He had realized that sometimes an ordered outside seeps within, just as sometimes a forced smiles makes a mood and standing up tall creates confidence.

This insight also reveals something fundamental about ritual: it is often the mechanism by which the world as it is experienced is reconciled with the ideal that is imagined or desired. Rituals may be external actions but they shape your internal perspective. Rituals allow you to bridge the world as it is with the world as you wished it was.

For many people, wine becomes a symbolic marker for the world as we wish it was; a world in which fine wine flows like natural springs. Wine in our culture is associated with gourmet food, especially rich cheeses and artisan breads; it is hard to even conceive of what wine goes best with greasy fish and chips. Wine life is imagined to have its own leisurely pace; rushing through a bottle of wine seems almost oxymoronic while pounding shots of vino as your friend does a barrel stand beside you certainly has no place in Burgundy. Rather, wine is perceived as a natural product; even the most manipulated wine is in the end a naturally-fermented fruit juice. For experienced wine drinkers, wine often evokes lazy days of wine tasting with friends in the countryside and past euphoric tasting experiences. People imagine a wine life that may differ by place and person, but it nearly always forms an ideal for them. As Robert Mondavi once said, "wine is the art of life itself."

This connection between wine and the good life is longstanding and cross-cultural: the ancient Greek historian Thucydides wrote that "the peoples of the Mediterranean began to emerge from barbarism when they learned to cultivate the olive and the vine." Throughout the bible, wine is the paramount symbol for God's blessings. The Patriarch of Israel, Jacob, promises his son Judah that the "foal will be tied to the vine…he will wash his garments in wine and his cloths in the blood of grapes." (Genesis 49:11) Apparently, you know god has blessed you when you have enough wine to wash your clothes in it. Blessings in ancient Judaism were often connected with wine, such as this one in the book of Proverbs: "That your barns will be filled with plenty and your vats burst out with new wine." (Proverbs 3:10) By contrast, a land without vines is a sign of a cursed land: The prophet Isaiah warns, "The wine dries up, the vine languishes, all the merry-hearted sigh." (Isaiah 24:7)

In the Christian New Testament, when Jesus wants to reveal himself, he compares himself to the vine (John 15:1) and the Kingdom of God to a vineyard. Even the normally tee totaling Muslims saw a wine-drenched world as a blessing from God: "I will leave all reason and religion behind and take the maidenhead of wine for mine, for wine is the grace of the Lord of the world."[6] Of course, through all these traditions, drunkenness may be depicted as negative and destructive but the goodness of the Creator nevertheless shines forth in wine-filled lands and wine-dark seas.

When the reality of our world gets us down, the ideal of the wine world comes to act as a panacea and remedy for despair. The rituals of wine are keys that open familiar doors of the mind that are filled with positive associations. To bring out your favorite corkscrew, open a bottle that you purchased at the vineyard, pour it deliberately into the perfect glass, take in its bouquet, examine its color like a kaleidoscope, and finally sip in its flavors—this ritual process marks the beginning of a journey for wine devotees away from the world as it is and toward the world as they wish it to be. The rituals of opening a wine become cues that you are now stepping away from the tensions found in your work or home life and are transported to your last trip to Napa or the cruise down the rivers of Bordeaux. The wine key becomes the cue to remember that life need not be like it is found in the present.

This desire to find refuge in a wine lifestyle is partially what draws people to wine festivals and grand tastings. For most attendees, these events are not trade shows hawking the latest products but rather opportunities to live in a world, albeit only for a few hours or days, in which wine flows freely, gourmet food abounds, and everyone shares your interests. For this reason, they are usually held in luxurious resorts or grand ballrooms, not convention centers. They include gourmet meals expertly paired with exclusive wines. For wine devotees, they are an escape from their everyday lives to experience oenological heaven, while still on earth.

The French sociologist Fischler notes that within the wine world, there are two distinct personalities: the *boire froid* (the cold drinker) is analytical and clinical, seeking to identify the faults of a wine; by contrast, the *boire chaud* (the warm drinker) seeks to find in the wine his/her hopes, desires, fantasies, and dreams.[7] This role for wine ritual is for the latter: those who find in their glass what they don't find in their world. Wine rituals become cues shift their internal world. As with my surfer student, it is the equivalent to putting on a dress suit to order a world that seems only to offer chaos. It temporarily shifts your mind's home address to the back roads of the Barossa, the Châteaus of Bordeaux, or the hillsides of Piedmont. There, the world might just be perfect, at least after a couple of glasses.

Forging Community through Wine Rituals

Every autumn, the roads to my university become filled for a day or two with processing groups of young women dressed in white holding candles and singing songs. Their neophytes stand among them, looking serious and somewhat scared at the rite that is about to unfold before them in the middle of night far away from public view. There are rumors about what happens in those ceremonies but they are always just rumors as the participants pledge secrecy to the grave. These young women are entering into the Greek mysteries; they are losing their identity and gaining a new one; they are becoming sorority sisters.

Fraternities and sororities, staples of American university life, are one of the last bastions of high-ritual left in an America in which every day is now casual Friday. While churches are informal and laid back, the frat and sorority houses still carry on the rituals of rush, pledge day, initiation rites, sacred oaths, secret handshakes, traditional songs, pins and paddles, vestments with sacred signs, candle ceremonies, altars, and a host of other elements that would look at home in a religious environment. The famed religious studies scholar at UC Santa Barbara Ninian Smart used to say that the fraternities were the most religious looking thing on campus, except that instead of bread and wine as their sacred feast, they have beer and pizza. However, this example reveals one of the most important staples of ritual: the forging of a close-knit group.

Rituals in religion are often tools to create and preserve group identity. The church, mosque, or temple is a place of congregation, where the people gather around the sacred. While rituals vary dramatically, they often communicate the shared values of the group: Catholics know their theology because of reciting the Creed each week; Muslims learn about equality by standing side-by-side during Friday prayers; Tibetans teach the value of the Dalai Lama to their children by burning incense as he passes. In rituals, the community learns what it means to be a part of the community. As the acclaimed anthropologist Edmund Leach observed, "We engage in rituals in order to transmit collective messages to ourselves."

At a bare minimum, a ritual bonds the people together in shared action, no matter how strange or meaningless the action may seem. One ashram in India I know has their disciples wear all white robes each night when they congregate together, bounce up and down and repeatedly shout "Boo"! The goal is to forge a common identity and affirm that identity through shared action. Ritual is the active engine for the creation of a community.

Wine rituals also serve to initiate and convey membership in a tribe. As you move from being a wine beverage consumer to a wine devotee, you learn the secret handshakes of the fraternity: open wine with a wine key, not a fancy electronic device; check the cork for signs of poor storage; hold the glass by the base or stem, not the bowl; generally drink pinots before zins in a tasting line up; etc... While there may be practical reasons for some of these rituals, they also provide a shared language and symbolic world for the community of wine devotees. Wine devotees marks their membership in the club through their reliable performance of wine rituals.

Understanding the role of rituals in forming community membership is important for deciphering even common interactions within the world of wine. For example, at wine events and tasting rooms, the ritual of discussing the wines with one another is central to the experience. Strangers will turn to one another: "Do you get green pepper on the nose of this cabernet?" Occasionally, the questioner is genuinely curious, but part of the motivation is to gauge whether the respondent is part of the wine club. Do they know that certain cabernet regions are (in)famous for green pepper aromas? Will they know that it often reveals less ripe wines? Will the responder offer their own coded sign that they are part of the club, such as the recognition that the 2015 Paso Robles cabernets tend to particularly reveal green pepper? On the surface, the questioner may seem like a detective in a crime of sensory evaluation but under the surface, the goal is identifying other people in the community of wine devotees.

In the global, individualized environment of the modern world, rituals seem like a hold-over from the past for most young people. They appear arbitrary, empty, archaic, and oppressive to self-expression. My students want to chart their own course, not follow the traditions of the past. They want to be more like Mollydooker and less like Burgundy; that is, until they taste Burgundy. More than one student has informed me that it would be more efficient if wine came in cans and drunk like beer. Such thinking misses the point for it still judges a ritual based on its practical value toward consuming a beverage. Wine rituals, however, create bonds of connection and inclusion between people; we reveal our "jersey" by the way we handle and speak about the wine around others. When I hold my glass a certain way, I am telling everyone in the room "I am not just drinking beverages like the bridal party at the end of the tasting bar but am part of the international brotherhood of wine believers." Like the rituals of sororities and fraternities, they may seem arbitrary and petty but they offer belonging and community. Be not afraid. You are not alone. This is the final message of wine rituals.

Chapter 4:
The Mysticism of Wine

"When people realize that wine is more than alcohol, it will be a more important step for humanity than going to the moon," Anne Morrey told me in an underground Burgundian cellar lined with bottles covered with dust and laden with history. Anne is a young *vigneron* (literally, wine grower) in an ancient land. Her family has been making wine around Meursault since the 17th century. She had her first wine when she was one hour old; it was a grand cru Montrachet. She now produces some of the smoothest white wines on the planet. She spoke these words not as if she hoped to shock or provoke me but rather like she was revealing a secret—a secret protected by some ancient Burgundian fraternity (a veritable Di***vin***ci code with wine at the center, which it happens to be since *vin* is wine in French). The phrase stuck in my mind for days afterwards.

"When people realize that wine is more than alcohol, it will be a more important step for humanity than going to the moon."

Although articulated differently and usually whispered late in the evenings through purple-stained lips, this sentiment is shared by wine devotees around the globe. Wine devotees know a secret about wine: it is more than alcohol, it is a pathway to Transcendence. They know this because they have experienced it themselves and that experience changed their lives. Simply stated, wine is meaningful for devotees because it has offered people meaningful experiences that other arenas in life do not. This chapter is an exploration of these experiences.

After talking with many wine devotees, I was immediately struck how similar their descriptions of their wine experiences are to religious mystics, who also have profound, transformative, and transcendent experiences. Moreover, the impulse that led mystics to fast regularly, contemplate sacred scriptures, and pray/meditate frequently in the hopes of a mystical experience is also found in the wine devotee who methodically tastes hundreds of wines, pours assiduously over vintage reports, and meditates over a glass in the hopes of having a transcendent wine experience. The two experiences diverge insofar as the wine experience does not lead to a sense of unity or a loss of self (well, perhaps *enough* wine could lead to a loss of self), but nevertheless the tools for analyzing mystics that have been developed for decades within my field are useful in making sense of these pinnacle wine experiences. For many people in the modern world, an encounter with a transformative and transcendent wine may just be the closest thing most people get to a mystical experience.

Understanding Traditional Religious Mystics

While mystics were once the everyday heroes and celebrities of the medieval world, today they seem so out of place that they need an introduction. Mystics across time and place are those that crave a direct, intimate encounter with an otherworldly Source. We will refer to this Source as God, but it is not necessary to picture only the masculine, Western God of Abraham because mysticism is also found in the East, where the Source may be known as the Mother Goddess, a Celestial Bodhisattva, or even the impersonal Dao. The mystic hopes to meld and merge with an otherworldly Source. Such an encounter occurs beyond the senses and far from reason. It is profound, deep, and life-altering.

In fact, words and rational discourse only get in the way and miss the point altogether. I often ask my students to imagine their perfect food. I then let my students in on a secret that, objectively, the perfect food is Twix Ice Cream. After years of letting this secret slip, I know that only a chosen few have tasted it, so I try to describe it to them and to you now. Truthfully, a thorough description would take pages but let me summarize the experience of tasting Twix Ice Cream in a few sentences: its base is a creamy vanilla that coats your mouth in velvety waves of full-fat goodness; the cream is cut by savory shortbread cookies that provide stomach-filling grains of a hearty meal; layers of chocolate then hit your palate like a surprising sunset on a rainy day; and finally, like the crash of a cymbal at the pinnacle of a great orchestral movement, sweet caramel springs forth unexpectedly. When all four of these flavors occur in a single bite, the result is not short of culinary magic. However, no matter how precise my description may be, no matter how poetically I describe my feelings, nothing can compare to a single bite of Twix Ice Cream. The mystics feel the same. We can dedicate all our efforts to talking about and analyzing God—we can even describe Him with the most sublime poetry—but nothing can replace 'tasting' Him directly for just one moment. It is not enough to love God from a distance or merely follow His rules; one should seek to lose oneself in Him. And if one does, even for a moment, one's life can never be the same again.

Transcendent wines can spark a similar profound journey. They untether us from our terrestrial view and show us vantage points within the mystery of life that we didn't know previously existed. They offer us an epiphany, which lexically means from Greek, the bringing of a light (*phanos*) upon (*epi*) someone. In this way, they are transcendent, uplifting us beyond the fragile ego we erect around us for security so that we see far beyond what we previously knew possible. Indeed, they make us confront our own smallness. Or perhaps such a realization of our insignificance is a natural result of being made aware of both of the thunderous vastness spilling out in time/space as well as the quiet power that forms the energy of the cosmos. In French, they call it an *éveil,* an awakening, for all life before seems like a slumber. We cannot be the same, nor do we want to.

The Spirit of Wine

Transcendent wines touch a different faculty of perception than even great wines, which can themselves go beyond the brute senses to engage the brain and the heart. Transcendent wines seek the soul or spiritual essence of a person.[1] The brain is too logical and heart too small to respond to the message of transcendent wines and so the message travels deeper within us. Indeed, not all people are prepared for such a transformative experience. But for those who are, wine becomes a divine river or liquid Dao or whatever formulation you want to give to something that offers an umbilical cord to unspeakable mysteries. Wine becomes not just alcohol but something that can transform the world more than going to the moon.

Both sides of this comparison between wine devotees and mystics will probably be offended by the argument contained in this chapter. To the mystic, wine lovers are worldly drunks who shun the spirit for the body; to the wine devotee, the mystic is a religious fanatic who rejects the things of the earth such as wine in favor of some nebulous, never-never spirit land. Yet, as we will see below, the mystics have historically turned to wine to describe their encounter with God and wine devotees often turn to language more appropriate to the monastic cell than a tasting room to capture their experience with the great bottles of wine.

They also share a struggle to make others understand them. Just as many people are puzzled by the passion and dedication of the religious mystic, so likewise there is frequently skepticism for those who gaze into the world of serious wine devotion. However, the response of the mystic and the wine devotee is the same: if doubters could only taste what I taste and feel what I feel during these heightened experiences, they would understand and their doubt would disappear. They will see that there is so much more to life, not just wine, than they now know. And when humanity realizes this, it will be a more important step than going to the moon.

The Four Elements of a Wine Mystical Experience

The skepticism regarding the potential mystical experience from wine deserves an arbitrator. William James, a 19th century philosopher and among the founders of psychology, might be a worthy candidate. Others often commented that he had mystic sensibilities, perhaps due to his relationship with his godfather Ralph Waldo Emerson and his brother, the author of the novel *Portrait of a Lady,* Henry James. William himself travelled the world and became convinced that mysticism was the common source of all religions. He argued that there are four common elements to the mystical experience that are consistent throughout all religions, throughout all eras, throughout all corners of the globe: passivity, transience, noetic, and ineffability. For wine experiences to count as mystical, they should fit these characteristics.

1. Passivity

Born of a wealthy family, St Francis of Assisi had a vision in 1204 that led him to give away all his earthly possessions so he could wander the countryside serving the poor and lepers.

74

He founded a way of life called mendicancy, which is derived from the word for beggar, because he wanted to return the church to its original goals of simplicity, poverty, and evangelism. For himself, he had but two requests for God: first, he wanted at least once to feel the overwhelming love for humanity that Jesus felt, and secondly, he wanted to experience the pain and suffering that Jesus endured during his Passion. Sure enough, one day while praying in a garden, he saw a vision of the Seraphim and he began to feel a piercing sensation on his wrists and ankles. Surprised, he looked down to discover the stigmata, the wounds of Christ appearing spontaneously. It was the ultimate mystical identity with Jesus, fully inscribing Jesus' suffering on his own body.

This story reveals something indicative of all mystical experiences: no matter how much one has prepared oneself or hopes for it, the mystic cannot force a mystical experience but rather it is something that comes upon him or her. In fact, it is now considered axiomatic that the mystical experience must be passive to be authentic. This realization does not mean that the mystic does nothing. Francis lived in extreme poverty and bodily mortification and he prayed continually, but nevertheless he could not make the stigmata happen by his actions. It came upon him suddenly and unexpectedly. Likewise, a mystical experience is something that happens to the mystic, even if he or she cultivates conditions that they hope will be conducive to it. The things one often associates with mystics—extreme bodily mortification, prayer, meditation, etc… –are never seen as the goal of the mystics or a mechanism to inevitably induce the experience but rather vehicles that create conditions in which a mystical experience is more likely to happen. Mysticism is a gift from the other side, however that Giver is conceived.

A transcendent wine experience is similar. You can't make them happen and in fact every wine connoisseur knows more the experience of a supposedly great bottle of wine that only disappoints than its opposite. It is not to say that you can't put yourself in a position to be *more* likely to have a transcendent experience with wine. Part II of this book offers a program for putting yourself in a position to have such experiences. Nevertheless, it is common sense that the experienced wine connoisseur is more likely to have transformative and transcendent wine experiences just as a monk who regularly prays, fasts, and performs daring acts of bodily mortification is more likely to have a mystical experience.

Likewise, the immediate environment can make a difference: if your first taste of La Tâche is on a Burgundy hillside surrounded by a kaleidoscope of colors on a surprisingly sunny autumn day with a new love, you are more likely to have a transcendent wine experience, but none of these elements are guarantees. It is also possible that on that hillside the wine will be corked, a close encounter with fire ants will leave a mark, or a fight with a surly lover will ruin the experience. In fact, most people's transcendent wine experiences come as a surprise, not from calculated plans.

The common phrase that one is bitten by the wine bug is not an accident; the devotee did not seek out a bug by which to be bitten but rather it came like a sudden illness that they couldn't deny and were powerless to deflect. More often than not, wine devotees admit that they did not choose a life of wine but rather the life of wine chose them.

And thus, the mystical wine experience is felt like a gift. As the famed Burgundian importer Becky Wasserman reminded me, every wine has a window in time when it is at its best as it traverses its long journey to becoming vinegar; there is some moment in a fine wine's life when it has perfect harmony and balance. We can fantasize about a contraption for wine like a turkey button that pops out when the bird is perfectly cooked but the fact is that no one know when that ideal moment to drink a wine has arrived. That is why when it does work, it feels like a gift.

Drink by charts provide educated guesses but one never knows when one opens a bottle if the target has been struck; you are at the mercy of past karma, fate, or providence. One can buy a wine directly from the cellar door, store it meticulously in perfect conditions, and serve it in a glass designed by scientists to capture the character of the varietal but none of this is a guarantee that the experience will be transcendent. Sometimes, it seems, the wine gods deliver and sometimes they don't. Mature wine drinkers learn to surrender or they quickly go crazy. Given the number of disappointing bottles, perhaps wine devotees are some of the most faithful people left on the planet.

Many people with the means to afford it have attempted to induce the experience by arranging tastings of legendary wines. Although few will mention it out loud, more often than not they fail to produce the mystical experience with wine any more than a week's fasting and prayer will produce a mystical experience for a monk. The wines are appreciated, but not transformative. Rather like the long-anticipated over-planned date, the anticipated feeling rarely lives up to reality. Buddhism might provide an explanation for this familiar let-down.

One of the cardinal virtues of Buddhism is a stress on being in the present. Humans so often are lost to dreams of the future, rehashing of the past, and fantasies of worlds that don't exist. When we plan every detail of the future and rehearse in our mind our expectations for how we will feel when that future event arrives, we create a movie in our head in which we are the central actor. As we dream of that future event, we are essentially rehearsing our future role. So, we imagine what we will feel when we taste that 1953 Petrus or 1870 Montrachet. When the time finally arrives, we begin to act our role and expect the movie to play out precisely like the preview we've seen so many times in our head; similarly, imagined proms always are better than actual proms.

As a result, when the event occurs, we are not mindful of the present. We become so busy acting that we are not aware of the Presence that can only be found in the present. There is the hope to have the experience but not the receptivity of the soul to appreciate it. There is an attempt to control and induce, rather than merely being open to the possibility of receiving a gift.

The authentic wine lovers are more like villagers on the island of Ios in Greece, a place where I frequented regularly when I was younger. Every evening, the whole island shuts down and the population climbs the hillside to watch the sunset. It is a routine, for certain, but they climb every night in the hopes of seeing something that touches them deeply. On the way up, you can overhear the locals pointing to signs that this evening might be special: the clouds are just right, the sky is exceptionally clear, the wind is coming from the right direction. However, having joined them for many of these, these are only educated guesses. They know that this is ultimately a passive experience; they sit and wait to see what God draws in the sky that evening for them. And when the last sliver of the sun disappears into the Aegean, they leave, some days after a collective slumping humph, some days after a thunderous applause, and some days after stunned silence because no one can speak in the face of such beauty.

Like the mystic and the wine devotee, they come away with the realization that sometimes we receive a gift of beauty, rather than create it. Transcendent wine experiences are a lot like the sunsets for the people of Ios. We can read all the signs and hope for the best, but ultimately having a transformative experience is beyond our control. Embracing this passivity is perhaps one of the most enduring lessons the gods of wine teach us.

2. Transience
When I was twenty-two, I had my first transcendent experience on a hillside at sunset on the monastic peninsula of Mt. Athos. I am still not sure if it should be categorized as

mystical but the land appeared to glow and waves of peace flowed across me like a gentle breeze through prairie grass. My instinct was to try to capture it. I took pictures. I recorded my impressions on a cassette tape. I tried to describe it in a miserable poem to a friend. I wished out loud that it wouldn't stop. But mystical experiences are live performances that must end and can never really be captured. My pleading did nothing and all my attempts at recording it were just embarrassing afterwards. Such is the nature of mystical experiences: they are finite, unrepeatable experiences. Even though you wish they would last forever, they tend to be brief, intense, and then pass, all without asking you what you want. No matter how hard you try, you cannot hold onto them. In fact, they become like sand in the hands of a child or snow ball on a hot day: the tighter you try to hold onto them, the more likely they are going to slip through your fingers. Sometimes you learn that holding tight means letting go.

Transcendent wine experiences are similar. Participants usually recognize them as they are happening and wish they could stop time but they can't. You could try to record them with the most poetic tasting notes, but we know that even live recordings of concerts never capture the energy of being present. So transcendent wine experiences come and they inevitably go with as much ease as they arose.

Perhaps real-time encounters of all kinds are like this but the transient character in wine is particularly marked because the wine is constantly changing from the minute you open it, especially if it is an aged bottle. If you are having a transformative experience with a wine immediately upon opening, it is almost guaranteed be a different experience in a half-hour as the wine is exposed to oxygen. Sometimes the oldest bottles seem to change in cycles of minutes if not seconds. By contrast, think of a transformative encounter with a work of art. A great work of art may have a meaningful impact on someone and the experience is likewise transient; the feeling one has will inevitably fade. However, the art does not change during the course of the experience, only the person perceiving it. In wine, both the person and the object are constantly changing and so there exists a dynamism in the transformative character of wine that is nearly unique.

The passive and transient character of the wine experience means that truly transformative wine events tend to be rare. The grandfather of Napa wine, Andre Tchelistcheff, was famous for saying that you should hope to have ten truly great bottles of wine in your life. Perhaps he is optimistic, at least on my budget. However, the relative infrequency is part of what drives the passion for wine. The desire for transformative and transcendent wine experiences is rarely if ever satisfied. Thus, there is always the hope that the next bottle will be the one that surprises, even if we know that it is unlikely going to be one of the handful of wines that are transcendent.

A similar process seems at work in the game of golf. Serious golfers, whose fanaticism toward their sport make wine obsession seem amateurish, are a masochistic bunch. They go through hole after hole often without hitting a shot with which they can be happy. But every once in a while, for reasons that usually aren't always apparent, every serious golfer will hit a nearly perfect ball. As long as they have one such shot a round, their fanaticism is kept alive because they know that it is possible; it is only a matter of time and practice, they reason, that every ball will be hit perfectly. Yet it is the relative rarity of the event that stokes the passion and keeps it fresh. Wine devotees are similar. They might drink through multiple cases before having a great wine and perhaps years before having a truly transcendent one. Yet, as long as they happen regularly enough, the passion is stoked and kept fresh. If the events were more frequent, their passion would not be so intense.

3. Noetic

In the Roman Empire of the Second Century, a movement known as Gnosticism argued that a spark of divinity existed within some people, known as the Elect. The rest of the people were literally godless and thus trapped in the flesh, which was destined to become their tomb. Perhaps sadder, however, was that many of the Elect lived unaware of the divinity within them, stuck in a prolonged sleep or stupor. The highest God, often called the One, does not want this situation to stand and so he sends down a messenger to awaken the Elect to their divine calling. This messenger, who is usually identified with Jesus in Gnosticism's Christian form, will provide the Elect with the intuitive knowledge, or gnosis, that allows the Elect to wake up and realize their divine identity within, see the divine source, and understand his plan for the cosmos. Without being awakened to Reality, they will

perish along with the fleshly.[2] Salvation for the Elect comes
through discovering who they are in dramatic moments of
gnosis, true knowledge.

Mystical encounters in all traditions work on similar
principles to Gnosticism. They extract you from your normal
existence, rearrange your internal world to reveal Reality and
the Real you, and then deposit you back where you were,
never to see the world in the same way again. A great wine
can lead to such gnosis. Becky Wasserman, the grand dame
of the Burgundy wine trade, describes her first encounter
with a 1945 La Tâche in a Vienna restaurant in the 1970s as,
"The world stopped and I was taken out of this world and
into a new consciousness." In Gnostic terms, Becky found in
that pinot a spark of divinity that engendered a new
framework for seeing the world. Perhaps only the Elect will
ever taste a 1945 La Tâche but her description of a new
consciousness gained by wine is surprisingly common, even
for those of us who assume that we are part of the fleshly
masses.

Here is how such a claim works: great wines lead us outside
ourselves to a place where we hereto forth did not know
existed. Whether we realize it or not, we all make maps of
the world that provide us meaningful existences by arranging
the things we know about the world into consistent frames
and structures. When we encounter a new piece of life data,
we place it onto this map; otherwise, we feel adrift. The
effect of great wine is that it demonstrates the inadequacies of
our existing maps for making meaning. We come to see that
the boundaries of our old maps were too narrow or our place

within the map misconstrued or the very vectors that orient us were off. Regardless of its specific form, we are awakened to a new way of seeing the world and we cannot return to the old one; once the window pane through which we see the world is shattered, we cannot put it back again. Our lives are forever transformed or so wine devotees and mystics claim.

Having interviewed hundreds of people who have experienced transcendent wines, no one has mentioned discovering unknown wine deities at the bottom of the bottle let alone the key for deciphering the famously enigmatic AOC system in France. The lessons gained are not about their life in wine but their life itself. Perhaps this fact explains why wine devotees take their drinking so seriously. It is not merely a hobby as people often assume from the outside, but a vehicle for discovering the meaning of life. Perhaps this observation helps explains Anne Morrey's comment with which we began this chapter. When people come to see wine as more than alcohol, they will discover it as a teacher in the art of life. If they do, it will perhaps be the most popular teacher the world has ever known.

4. Ineffable (Indescribable)

When academic historians came together to produce a list of the 100 most influential people in history, most people assumed that Jesus, the founder of the world's largest religion, would occupy the top spot. In actuality that honor went to the founder of the second biggest religion, Muhammad, and Jesus fell to the third spot after Isaac Newton. Historians are not anti-Christian but rather argued that despite Jesus' importance to Christianity, the religion as we know it is due nearly as much to the Apostle Paul, who occupies sixth on the list. It is no exaggeration to say that without Paul, we would not have Christianity, at least as we know it. And we wouldn't have Paul without a mystical experience that transformed from an ardent persecutor of Jesus and his movement to its most ardent and articulate defender. Here is how the Apostle Paul himself describes it in 2 Corinthians 12:1-5

> *I must go on boasting. Though there is nothing to be gained by it, I will go on to visions and revelations of the Lord. I know a man in Christ who fourteen years ago was caught up to the third heaven—whether in the body or out of the body I do not know, God knows. And I know that this man was caught up into paradise—whether in the body or out of the body I do not know, God knows— and he heard things that cannot be told, which man may not utter. On behalf of this man I will boast, but on my own behalf I will not boast, except of my weaknesses.*

If Paul turned this description to me as a college essay, he would not have received a high mark and the marginal note would read in bold letters: "Be specific!" However, the problem is not with his writing style but the nature of mystical experiences. The mystical experience is so profound, so otherworldly that ordinary language struggles when trying to describe it. Paul may want to share the experience with others but language seems to falter when pressed to these other-worldly duties and so he adds all those awkward phrases reflecting that struggle. Paul is not alone. All mystics struggle to describe their mystical experience because by nature they appear to be ineffable or at least defying easy expression. Language is too this-worldly to describe something fundamentally otherworldly.

Rather than admit that their experience is something that cannot be described (and thus any language about it borders on non-sense), mystics have developed a series of linguistic strategies to convey to others a sense of an experience fully beyond the senses. Poetry is perhaps the most common approach because its reliance on metaphor and symbol perform well at pointing to the experience without directly expressing it. Poets paint in broad strokes and evoke families of images rather than get bogged down in precise linguistic formulations.

Drunkenness is a common theme in mystic poems, as we shall see below, but the favorite genre of mystical poetry is eroticism, which is particularly apt in describing the union the mystics felt. Perhaps it is easier to explain the union in terms most people know or at least fantasize about. The author of the Songs of Solomon can describe his love for the God of Abraham in terms that the editors at Harlequin will envy: "You have ravished my heart with a glance of your eyes, with one jewel of your necklace... Your lips distill nectar, my bride; honey and milk are under your tongue...Your channel is an orchard of pomegranates ....a garden fountain, a well of living water, and flowing streams...." A sort of literary liberty is granted to erotic poetry for it is all metaphor in this case, no matter how fleshly it seems.[3]

Paradox is also at home in poetry. The fourth century Eastern Christian Gregory of Nyssa describes his direction encounters with God as occurring in a "dazzling darkness" or in "thunderous silence" with "sober inebriation" or "passionless passion." Here language is a tool that leads us beyond reason, where the mystical encounter resides. Perhaps the most developed expression of this approach is found in the Zen koans or riddles. These are logical conundrums that rattle the mind and expand its parameters. The most famous of which is: "Two hands clap and there is a sound; what is the sound of one hand?" Even a glass of wine won't help solving that dilemma, but it can't hurt.

James' observation regarding the ineffability of the mystical experience is undoubtedly accurate, but one also has to admit that mystics do not let it remain that way. Mystics are voluminous describers. If the goal of the mystic is to "taste" god then they write some of the longest tasting notes in history. Herein begins our connection to wines, especially transcendent wines. The very nature of the transcendent wine experience is that it eludes precise language. They are the wines that leave us speechless. Their profundity is apparent by the resultant ineffability. The Burgundy Evangelist Allen Meadows captures this struggle with words well:

> When the pursuit of vinous perfection finally leads you to a glass containing a wine of flawless resplendence, it is a powerful and unforgettable encounter. I would imagine it being akin to having seen the face of an angel and then immediately wondering what to do with that knowledge. Do you try to tell others what you have "seen"? Or do you

accept, grudgingly, that the experience cannot be
adequately captured by words alone because they are
inherently too limited to completely describe a
transient experience? Discussing each element in a
perfect wine is like trying to pick out the individual
dabs of color in a Pointillist painting. The sum of the
individual parts never quite equals the seamless
perfection of the whole.[4]

As with the challenge of describing an angel to the spiritually
deaf, the wine devotee struggles to put the pieces together
into a coherent narrative. However, as Meadows notices, the
ineffable experience is not just the sum of its underlying parts
but acts more like a puzzle than a beacon of clarity. We
should probably just stay silent, but we can't.

The problem is even more difficult for wine than perhaps
even traditional mystical experiences for reasons that may
need some explanation. Languages work because there is
mutually-agreed upon referents corresponding to certain
letter combinations or sounds. So, when we combine the
letters y-e-l-l-o-w together, we all roughly know the
corresponding region on the color spectrum to which it
refers. Tying to describe the meaning of yellow to a color-
blind society would be a challenge precisely because they have
not experienced it. Part of the challenge of the traditional
mystic in conveying his/her experience to others is that most
people have not had the experience and thus tying to describe
a mystical experience is like describing yellow to a land that is
color blind. We simply don't have the shared vocabulary to

describe a supra-rational, supra-sensational experience that only a relative few have experienced.

At this point, one might think that the wine devotee is at an advantage compared to the traditional mystic because while most people have not tasted a transcendent wine, most people have tasted wine and so at least know the general terrain of a great wine. However, our natural faculty for taste is far more varied across people than our other senses. It is not just that three people tasting a wine will have different aesthetic and quality judgments—in fact, they likely will—but rather that these three people may actually taste the wine differently because of physiological differences. Some people are genetically predisposed to be more sensitive to temperature while others are predisposed to discriminate difference more finely but perhaps the largest difference lies with the supertasters.[5] Supertasters perceive bitterness and sweetness more intensely than normal tasters, in part because they have more taste buds per square centimeter than others.[6] It does not mean that they are better tasters but it does mean that they are different tasters.

Likewise, environmental factors such as the time of day, recently consumed foods, the amount of sleep, and a whole host of other factors shape the physical taste of the wine. Thus in all wine, but particularly complex wines such as those that make up transcendent wines, there is no guarantee of a common experience upon which to develop mutually-agreed upon linguistic referents. In other words, the wine devotee who is attempting to describe his/her mystical wine experience is doubly disadvantaged: not only is it an otherworldly experience that only a rare few have experienced but it depends in part on a subjective taste for which there is no guarantee of shared references. The best language can do is point to the experience but it never will encapsulate it. This is the insight, I think, of one of the modern masters of the science of wine tasting, the French professor Émile Peynaud, who concludes, "it is impossible to describe a wine without simplifying and distorting its image."[7] The same can be said of God.

Because of these inherent challenges, some people will argue that we should never describe our most profound wine experiences. "Smell it! Inhale the bouquet! Taste it! Drink it! But never try to describe it!" concludes the main character in Roald Dahl's short story "Taste." However, precious few are silent wine drinkers. Rather, we continue to try to share our wine experiences despite or perhaps because of the "the impossibility of pinning down the butterfly of taste in a linguistic aspic," in Nigel Bruce's evocative phrasing.[8] Attempting to describe them requires staring into the abyss and discovering a reimagined self. Words may ultimately fall short, but sharing that self with others is still scary as hell. Yet fear of hell has often been the start of religions.

Conclusion on Mystical Experiences

"The gods talk in the breath of the woods, They talk in the shaken pine, And fill the reach of the old sea-shore, With melody divine."[9] These words were penned by a mystic, but not a traditional one. They were written by Ralph Waldo Emerson, who together with his friend Walt Whitman, hoped to found a new religion grounded in the mystical encounter gained in nature. "I too, following many and follow'd by many, inaugurate a religion," Whitman declared, "…I say the whole earth and all the stars in the sky are for religion's sake."[10] They did not advocate prayer, fasting, or asceticism for their religion but seeking to find the divine though the beauty and complexity of nature. The mountains were their cathedrals and the woods their monasteries. At the time, few would have put them alongside the likes of classical mystics such as Gregory of Nyssa, Hildegard of Bingham, or St. Francis of Assisi. Yet nature eventually came to be recognized as a legitimate vehicle to go beyond oneself and touch the infinite.

Transcendent wines in the lives of wine devotees play the same role as nature did to Emerson and Whitman. Just as many people tromp through the woods without any sense of their potential for transcendence, so many people drink their plonk, unaware of wine's potential. For the rare few who have transcendent wine experiences, they act like traditional mystical experiences, at least as described by William James: they come unexpectedly upon the drinker who is passive; they are transient so that the person having it cannot hold onto regardless of any desires to the contrary; they are noetic in that they lead to previously unknown insights; and finally, they are ineffable, despite the impulse to describe them.

They may not *seem* like mystical experiences, even for those who have had them, but it is only because people had not tried to fit them into that category previously. The drinkers, now the wine devotees, only knew that they were changed because of their experience. Wine has transformed them.

They were given a beautiful gift through wine and they will search high and low for another transcendent and transformative wine. The search is one of the most ancient in religious history: the quest for the Holy Grail that promises metamorphosis and eternity. Fittingly, it will be a wine chalice.

Here is what Ann Morry of Montrachet meant, I think. Wine might always be known for its alcohol for some, but wine can be so much more than a means to achieve a buzz, when given the chance. Wine has the potential to transform humanity's consciousness. It has the power to extract people from their cocoons constructed by their ego and set them free to see the world from the perspective gained only by fluttering through the tree tops. Not all wines have this power, but certain wines drunk under the right conditions hold the potential to awaken people. Hoping that others have such an experience has been the call of religions from the beginning of time. It is the good news of the latest edition of the Gospel of Wine. When people embrace this message, it will be more important for humanity that going to the moon.

Epilogue on wine in the Mystics

"I will take one hundred barrels of wine tonight…I will leave all reason and religion behind and take the maidenhead of wine for mine, for wine is the grace of the Lord of the world….Piety and moral goodness have naught to do with ecstasy; stain your prayer rug with wine!"

These are the words of a mystic. Yet he is not a wine devotee but a traditional Islamic mystic: the ninth century Persian mystic Hafiz. His statement is all the stranger since the Quran forbids the drinking of wine, let alone hundreds of barrels of wine in a night; in fact, one of the penalties for drinking wine is an afterlife of total abstinence in which the sinner is forced to drink instead the putrid puss of prisoners in hell. Given the penalty, it better be good wine. But Hafiz is not alone among the mystics of the world to uphold wine. In the Christian West, St. Bernard (1090-1153) uses his mystical closeness with the Mother of God to plead the following: "Ah, tender Mother! Tell your all-powerful Son that we have no more wine. We are thirsty after the wine of his love, of that marvelous wine that fills souls with a holy inebriation, inflames them, and gives them the strength to despise the things of this world and to seek with ardor heavenly goods." One can't help wonder if he's had some practice at Holy inebriation. In Chinese thought Xiuxi Yin was one of the so-called Seven Sages of the Bamboo Grove, a group of Chinese scholars and poets of the mid-third century A.D. who advocated a new form of spirituality:

> During the 36,000 days of a century; one should drink 300 goblets of wine each day; Such pleasure, to enter the Land of Drunkenness; First sober, then drunk;

drunken and wild; Once we have gone into the hills, we can immediately forget about worldly affairs; In the sky there is a wine star, on earth a wine spring; from my walking stick I often hang a bag of coins. A pool of wine with a mound of wine sediment alongside brings me pleasure, so I whirl about and drunkenly dance; it is as if I am donning the feather cape, donning the feather cape and ascending into immortality. While in the cups I attain the Dao in a truly joyful manner.[1]

The Chinese poet declares that the Dao reside in wine glasses and he knew this without, presumably, even trying a fine Burgundy. These three cases from different places and times all raise the same question: what the hell is going on here? Why are these people, who are said to stand at the pinnacle of their spiritual traditions that generally eschew alcohol, praising wine and drunkenness so gallantly?

The key to deciphering this mystery lies in returning to James' fourth attribute of mystical experiences: their ineffability. These mystics have all had experiences that they consider indescribable and their challenge is to convey them to others. They need metaphors that are both graspable to the audience yet also convey some sense of an experience of going beyond oneself and offering a higher vision. Wine, the noblest of all beverages, does both. People knew wine (Persians were known for their wine consumption despite the Quran) but for our purposes the fact the mystics chose wine as a symbol of something that uplifts the soul is important. Of course mystics have used numerous different metaphors, but when they choose wine, they are presupposing that their audience

94

will at least have some glint of knowledge about its transcending potential. As far as I am aware, no mystic has declared: "Let me drink water until I am full of God!" or even "let me down whisky until I see God!" Rather, wine is employed because it has a transcending potential that other beverages do not. Wine can take you to the stars while other alcohol just makes you see them.

Yet, lest we come to think they are advocating libidinous consumption, the mystics are usually clear that they mean it strictly metaphorical. The Islamic mystic Ibn al-Farid notes that the wine of the mystics is pure wine, "eternally prior to all existing things" and made from an ethereal "vintage that made us drunk before the creation of the vine."[2] Apparently this is a wine that ages incredibly well. But the point is that it is a metaphor for a type of experience, not a call to start benchmarking Bordeaux. While spiritual drunkenness will receive more treatment later, the drunkenness is also a metaphor for the loss of self, in this case because one is so fully united with God. As a result, while the use of wine metaphors in the traditional mystics bears some similarity to the subject of this chapter, ultimately their uses diverge. For traditional mystics, wine is a metaphor for an experience cultivated through other means; for the wine devotee, spirituality is the metaphor for an experience cultivated through wine. In the former, wine is a form of poetry; in the latter, as Aubert de Villaine has argued, wine is the poetry.

Chapter 5:
Pinotphilia and The Religious Fanatics of the World of Wine

A vineyard manager in Burgundy is tending to the vines during vintage when a child carelessly mixes the pinot grapes with other lesser varietals from the vineyards. The year is 1393, twenty years after the appropriately-titled Philip the Bold had given pinot its name. Incensed at this act of pinot defilement, his rebuke takes the form of a beating so severe that the child dies. Eventually, the *maître de la vigne* was pardoned by a judge; after all, the judge wrote, it was pinot.[1]

This tragic event may have been long ago but it reflects the attitude of those caught by the Pinotphilia bug to the present. The degree of devotion to pinot surpasses all others. In the stuffy world of wine, it is the grape that makes otherwise demure tasters come to life in front of you with apoplectic verbal ejaculations recalling a particular Burgundy tasting like it was the discovery of fire. It is a grape that leads its initiates to study the intricacies of the byzantine designation system of Burgundy like they were cramming for the bar exam, (which is easier, by the way). For Pinotphiles, Romanée-Conti in Burgundy is their Xanadu, a natural cathedral where fellow pinot pilgrims fall to their knees. More than one pilgrim has been known to take a bit too literally the claim that the ancient monks of Burgundy used to taste the soil to appreciate its complexity. Indeed, the Passion of the pinot runs so deep even today that one suspects many of Pinotphiles would justify that first vineyard manager's infanticide in the name of pinot purity, and might even offer their own offspring.

The evangelical rhetoric around pinot is so zealous that it is seems like it is a path to material and spiritual bliss. "Pinot appeals to higher and base instincts," says one wine writer, "hijacking at once both the primordial amygdala and the evolved frontal cortex. A good pinot places you truly under her spell, you pass orgasm and go directly to post-coital bliss."[2] While some may argue that the latter promise is a shame, there is sort of noble hedonism found in pinot. Vanity Fair writer Joel Fleishman penned the following panegyric to pinot: "At their best, pinot noirs are the most romantic of wines, with so voluptuous a form so sweet an edge, and so powerful a punch that, like falling in love, they make the blood run hot and soul wax embarrassingly poetic." I couldn't agree more, for love of pinot is like a summer breeze that makes my soul shiver as fresh dew in the morning's rays.

The Spirit of Wine

I traveled once to the southern region of Burgundy to interview the famed chronicler of Burgundian wine, the English wine writer Clive Coates, with hopes to understand the appeal of pinot. He is typically British—reserved, slightly stuffy, and overly-polite in a sort of manner that one could imagine fitting in well in a colony. As we talked, it seemed as if his spiritual impulses had been muted by his life, as if not even years of drinking the finest wines in the world could loosen the straight-laced neck tie of history for him. Yet, when he writes on pinot, he melts into a sappy Romantic, such as in this passage: "[Pinot] is a wine which can sing like a nightingale, shine forth like a sapphire, intrigue like the most complex of chess problems and seduce like the first kiss of someone you are just about to fall in love with. Moreover, great burgundy can inspire like a great orator, satisfy like the subtlest of three-star meals, and leave you at peace at the end like the slow movement of a Mozart piano concerto. At its best, the wine is complex but not puzzling, profound but not didactic, perfect but not intimidating, and magnificent but never anything less than friends.[3]" Pinot can bring world peace. Perhaps not, but pinot here is a panacea of all life's problems and a liquid pathway to paradise. One gets the feeling that even the Gods would be jealous of pinot.

Yet, pinot is a jealous God for its adherents, who rarely will tolerate any competing allegiance. Historically, their ire has been directed at Bordeaux, for the Rhône or Piedmont are not even worthy to mention in the same sentence, let alone Napa or the Barossa Valley. The Burgundy apologist Oz Clarke writes "Even the most poetically conceived, even the most inspired in execution of red Bordeaux cannot make your heart race and your head swim with dreams and fantasy quite like great red Burgundy can. " This attitude arises in the famous summary of the French wine scene: "Burgundy makes you think of silly things, Bordeaux makes you talk of them and Champagne makes you do them."[4] The Burgundy apologists fancy themselves as the most refined of wine drinkers but in the era of the soundbite, these attacks seemed to have devolved into something more like trash talk than measured criticism. In a book on the rivalry, the author relays the current sentiment: "Bordeaux makes you piss. Burgundy makes you fuck."[5] Viva Burgundy!

Herein lies where the devotion to pinot becomes not just a consumer passion like beanie babies and pet rocks but eerily similar to religious fanaticism. One of the distinctive traits about religion is that most religious people are not cognizant of their role in choosing their religion. Religious people do not choose to be devotees, they are chosen. The myth of being the chosen ones is persistent across traditions. The Jews, of course, were the original self-proclaimed chosen ones but many other traditions share this notion. The term "church" that was adopted by the early Christians derived from two Greek words—*ek* (out) and *kleo* (to call) for the Christians saw themselves as those called out by God to be separate. Seventh-Day Adventists hold that they are the remnant, the ones chosen by God to survive the last days. The Ramanandis in India held that they alone were descendants of Lord Rama. Rastifarians hold that the whole black race was chosen by Jah, God incarnate. The Pinotphiles project this sort of purpose and will to pinot noir. They did not choose to love pinot but were "seduced" by the "siren song" of pinot; pinot "makes the blood run hot."

Pinot becomes personified as a jealous God who is reaching out to create its own believers.

Those that fall for pinot become part of the chosen nation of wine. In other words, I did not choose pinot but pinot chose me, and I am special because of it. The disciples of pinot all have a story. Jamie Kutch was a Wall Street trader until one night he had a particular pinot noir, a 2002 Kosta-Browne, and within weeks, he quit his job, moved to California, and began to dedicate his life to making pinot. Today, he is the winemaker at Kutch wines. Ray Walker worked in finance near San Francisco until he quit it all to eventually pursue pinot in Burgundy. Deb and Bill Hatcher visited Willamette from their home in St. Louis in 1985. Upon tasting a pinot there, they went home, packed up their belongings, and eventually started two labels that are now two of the biggest in the state.[6] These stories—and they could be multiplied easily—are classic tales of radical conversion. These are religious conversion stories, but it is by a particular grape, not a God. Or perhaps it is to them.

As with other forms of religious fundamentalism, Pinotphilia appears to be on the rise. After decades of declining quality, modern pinot devotion was resurrected after a legendary 1985 vintage. The 1990s brought the awakening of American pinot: supermarket sales tripled from 1993 to 1998; Californian pinot was growing at 15% a year; and the harvest in Oregon tripled in the decade from 1989 to 1998. Then came the movie Sideways, an extended Ode to pinot that did as much to halt the rise of merlot as it did to prop up pinot. Sales volume in the United States of pinot increased by 57 per cent in the immediate aftermath of the film's release. And we now see the spread of this fierce monotheism around the globe. Its conversion rate matches the Mormons but with an impact on the pocketbook closer to Scientology.

To justify this degree of devotion, Pinotphiles create a myth surrounding the grape that makes it unique, unlike nearly all other grape varietals. The myth states that pinot is the hardest grape to grow and the hardest wine to make. In one of the most famous odes to pinot, the lead character in the movie *Sideways* educates his agnostic friend:

> It's a hard grape to grow, as you know. Right? It's uh, it's thin-skinned, temperamental, ripens early. It's, you know, it's not a survivor like cabernet, which can just grow anywhere and uh, thrive even when it's neglected. No, pinot needs constant care and attention. You know? And in fact it can only grow in these really specific, little, tucked away corners of the world. And, and only the most patient and nurturing of growers can do it, really. Only somebody who really takes the time to understand pinot's potential can then coax it into its fullest expression. Then, I mean, oh its flavors, they're just the most haunting and brilliant and thrilling and subtle and...ancient on the planet.[7]

This is myth making in both senses of the word. It constructs a world of meaning that justifies a belief and it is only partially true. Physiologically, the bunches are tighter making it more susceptible to rot and it is (appropriately) thin-skinned, but it is not categorically dissimilar to other grapes. Likewise, making a pinot—or "taming the pinot"— as it is often deemed, is said to be fraught with difficulty: the lead wine critic of the New York Times once wrote, "If any grape would be at home in the pose of the femme fatale— smoke curling from its lips, long, irresistible legs crossed as another winemaker is sent to his doom—it would be pinot."[8]

Without doubt, pinot is finicky and may fret oxygenation but the winemaking process is not categorically any different from other grapes. Is it really worthy of being called the variety "from which suicides are made", as Australian critic James Halliday says?[9] Nevertheless, pinot description tends to the dramatic: "Burgundy is a minefield; you can be blown to hell or blown to heaven."[10] Perhaps precisely because of this quality, its reputation is so built up that it carries an allure that no other wine holds. In a book dedicated to pinot called *The Heartbreak Grape,* the author Marq De Villiers notes: "They called it the heartbreak grape because it was so stubborn, so particular, so elusive, so damn difficult to get right. And also because when it was at its best it made the most sublime wine of all. The heartbreak grape? You cannot break a heart without having captured it first."[11] This is the beauty of pinot—it loves you despite, or perhaps because of, its challenges.

This myth is surprisingly longstanding. In 1896, a respected U.C. Davis professor commented: "in some localities (of California) it is doubtless possible to make pinot Noir wine of high quality and to age it, but only with a minute attention to detail and an elaborate care, which no price that is likely to be obtained at present would justify."[12] There are some things money can't buy and decent pinot seems to be one of them, at least for the end of the 19th century. The result of such mythmaking is an allure that no other varietal can match.

One California pinot maker, Eleven Row, begins their promotional material by setting the stage: "Pinot Noir appeared in Burgundy around 6BC. For over one millennium, scholars, princes, soldiers, kings and Popes have traveled through the fabulous Cote d' Or, drinking and hearing and dreaming about the great wines found there." Despite the evident math challenges in this statement, the message is clearly that drinking pinot will make you the equivalent of royalty, you will be the one of the Chosen across time. But, the website adds, "Pinot Noirs are extremely temperamental. They are susceptible to just about everything. One minute they are beautiful and open, and the next moody and closed. For this reason, they are the hardest wines to make. But, when everything hits, they are in a world all their own."[13] It may take some self-flagellation to tame but the promise of paradise in a glass is worth it. You are buying not just fancy grape juice but a place in a mythic dream that spans across the ages. As the self-proclaimed Prince of Pinot concludes, "It's not the pinot in your life, but the life in your pinot that really counts."

This aspiration is the secret goal of many of the Pinotphiles. However, as with most religious believers, the goal is hidden from their conscious self by framing their devotion in terms of an objective pursuit of truth. Pinot is presented as a passageway to Truth, as the great Danish author Karen Baroness von Blixen-Finecke, also known as Isak Dinesen, once wrote, "There are many ways to the recognition of truth and Burgundy is one of them." Yes, Plato, Jesus, and pinot are merely parallel paths to Truth. Enlightenment comes from being open to the truth, as one winemaker from Oregon said, "Pinot Noir, more than anything, should tell the truth. And it does that very well. But you have to take a risk in order to hear the truth and then you might not always hear what you expect."[14] Salvation is not by grace alone but by the active seeking out of salvation by those who have faith. As one winemaker stated, "Burgundy has all the answers if you know to ask the right questions."[15]

Yet this pinot Truth is not a philosophical one but a spiritual one. Wine writer Matt Kramer is a bit sheepish, but he makes the case: "Even the most skeptical are willing, after savoring a genuinely great Burgundy, to concede that there may well be—dare one say it?—a Presence in the universe beyond our own."[16] This presence is not something discovered through the intellect or rational discourse. Rather, it is something felt in the heart, not the head. To paraphrase a traditional Islamic Sufi saying, "We will hang the intellect like a thief, when pinot comes to rule."

When the papacy was in France in the 14th century, one of the arguments against its return to Rome was that "there was no Beaune [a central city of Burgundy] in Italy" and the cardinals could not live without its wine, which they considered a "fifth element." William Shakespeare called it a "marvelous searching wine and it perfumes the blood ere one can say, "What's this?"[17] In more contemporary circles, the great Burgundy apologist Oz Clarke writes: "The flavours of the greatest red Burgundies are sensuous, often erotic, *above rational discourse and beyond the powers of measured criticism* as they flout the conventions in favour of something rooted in emotions and passions too powerful to be taught, too ancient to be meddled with.[18] The fact that pinot is presented as being "beyond rational discourse" is precisely the traits that breed nearly mystical devotion that borders on sheer irrational fanaticism. Pinot touches the soul and uplifts us into that spiritual insight that there is a "Presence in the universe beyond our own." Many Catholic priests wish communion would have such an effect; of course, if the chalice was full of pinot instead of communion wine, maybe it would.

Part II:
Becoming a Wine Devotee

Introduction

Kanzaki Shizuku, a young Japanese beer salesman, receives
news that his legendary wine-critic father has died.
Summoned to the family chateau for the reading of the will,
he learns that his eccentric father will make him earn his
inheritance by playing a high-stakes game of blind wine
tasting against a young, debonair critic with a legendary
palate. To receive his inheritance, Shizuku must correctly
identify twelve wines which the father has deemed the
"Twelve Apostles" and then a special thirteenth wine that
surpasses them all, known only as the "Drops of God."
Having never had a glass of wine before, Shizuku goes about
educating himself about the wines of the world. Soon, young
women swoon over his decanting skills and the way he pops
the corks. He is a natural. In the first wine showdown,
Shizuku correctly identifies the age, varietal, and origin of a
wine even though his only exposure to that particular grape
came from eating a handful of them as a child.

It is a classic tale of love for wine, women, and family but it is
not real: all this occurs within a popular Japanese manga
comic book called "Drops of God" which has become a best
seller in its French and English translations and is now a live-

action TV drama. It has a following of over 500,000 people and Decanter magazine called it "'arguably the most influential wine publication for the past 20 years." It also serves as a metaphor for the journey of wine devotees who have been the topic of this study: the process of learning about, consuming, and identifying wine becomes a spiritual task for them, a journey into God. Unlike direct revelation, however, it requires learning to see wine as an earthbound overflow of divinity, the drops of God.

Having examined the stages in the spiritual journey into wine, we now turn to understanding the mechanisms by which you can make wine more meaningful in your life. How do you transform the fruit of the vine into drops of God? While every spiritual journey is unique, there seems to be patterns with those who have turned to wine as their spiritual muse. Part II of the book is an exploration of some of these themes. Remember, however, that spiritual journeys are very personal so maybe not every suggestion in the follow pages will speak to you. It is fine. Move on and find what works for you. My hope is that sharing some of the ways wines have led to meaning in others' lives will be inspiration for you.

Becoming a Wine Devotee
Step 1: Cultivate Connection to the Wine

The Apostle Paul famously noted that Athens had an altar to an "unknown" God. I've always wondered who worshipped at that altar, but while we may never know, I doubt anyone had a transcendent experience there. Humans do not seem naturally inclined to be moved by something to which they cannot relate. The reason is simply that love, even with a deity, rarely occurs among strangers, at least the most meaningful kinds of love. It is not that one has to know everything about one's chosen deity, but one has to know enough to draw the whole person in. It seems like for this reason, all the gods in the global hall of fame—Yahweh, Allah, Krishna, etc...—have well-developed personalities that at times can seem surprisingly human-like. Wine functions in the same way. No one drinks wine in the abstract, but wine is only known through its particular forms, or more concretely, certain bottles. Each of these bottles has a biography, a story that allows us to relate. While it will not guarantee a moving wine experience, knowing that story can improve the likelihood of having a meaningful experience immeasurably.

All these suggestions presuppose that the wine is capable of conveying a story. An industrial wine that just says, "Red Table Wine of South Australia" has little likelihood of having a story or leading to a meaningful experience. Of course, just because a wine has a biography does not mean that it will be drinkable or contribute to your spiritual life; wine from the California Mission grape made by oenologically-incompetent monks for the tourist trade may have a story, but it is dreadful to drink. Yet, wines with biographies tend to be from smaller producers, have specific vineyard designations, and be made by winemakers who are reflective enough to want to share the story of its pedigree and birth with you. When wines are capable of this depth, they come alive to the drinker.

Learning the Biography of a Wine

Francois Millet is the "chef de cave" at the legendary Domaine Comte Georges de Vogüé in Musigny, Burgundy. When those of us in the new world dream of the old world, we imagine places like de Vogüé. It is an old stone building near a church in sleepy town, a quiet village where every day is like the one before, for centuries. Francois speaks nearly perfect English, yet still I found myself lost early on in our conversation. He seemed to be talking about Amoureuses, a woman in love. She is the first lady of the village, he told me, dolled up in the finest clothes and carrying herself regally. Yet she stands at a distance, never allowing us to embrace her.

The Spirit of Wine

We contemplate her rather than touch her. And when we do, we discover that she has sadness just below the layers of perfect make-up. She is affected by death, yet doesn't want to show it. Every year, she is somewhat different—or I should say every vintage, for I later realized that Amoureusus is a delicate red wine, not a person.

When we went down into the ancient cellars, we first tasted her husband, the Musigny (which also, by the way, demands contemplation) and then the crazy uncle by marriage, the Bonnes-Mares. By the time we reached the lady of the day, I must admit that I was skeptical of such anthropomorphism. Perhaps it was the power of suggestion, but I have never tasted a wine in quite the same way. It was not just analyzing something but communing with someone. She was alive. I felt underdressed around her and I instinctively straightened my posture. She drew me to her, not as a wine but as a person. It struck me for the first time that great wine has this capacity like few other non-human entities on earth.

As humans born of other humans, the default parameter for understanding relationships is human. As a result, our tendency is to humanize anything with which we have a meaningful relationship. Of course, the ability to anthropomorphize is strong—think of the pet rock craze of the 1970s and longstanding tradition of sailors naming and referring to their boats by female names. It is also a staple of religious worlds, such as when people depict God as a stern father or worship in front of anthropomorphic image of a divinity. There seems to be a direct correlation between the extent of anthropomorphization and the depth of relationship formed: the more one can imagine a relationship in human terms, the more significant the relationship has the capability of being. Here wine is nearly unique in the extent that it has become personified for people. Think about the human story of wine:

Each winter in a vineyard (that is itself usually given a name), an orgy of conception occurs with new grape clusters formed seemingly out of thin air. They begin small and fragile, but their cells multiply and they become sturdier over time. These clusters will eventually become the wine with whom we have a relationship, but we avoid getting too attached because one never knows the final outcome at this early stage. The wine is still in the womb at this point and those who are part of the process are filled with anticipation. A wine has what historian William Younger calls a "heaving" birth and indeed at one winery with which I am familiar, the fermentation room is called the birthing room.

The newly-birthed wine then goes through a period of infancy where it is kept in a protective space in a barrel until it is ready to grow up and be released to the world. At this point, we talk about the wine as we talk about infants and toddlers: their personalities are beginning to show but it is all potential. We final allow it to graduate and send it out into the world, hoping that we've prepared it to change in good ways but fearing that we might have done something that will lead to defaults or failures, some of which might not appear for many years.

We speak of the early years of a wine's release as being "young," which as with people, usually means excusably brash, immature, unsubtle, and still trying to find its way in the world. Unlike wine beverage drinkers, wine devotees

114

allow wine to mature. The collection of wine is critical because if one does not watch a wine develop throughout a case or over multiple vintages, then the relationship to wine is like a series of one-night stands: titillating but ultimately leaving one with an empty feeling. So, wine devotees look for connections across time: multiple bottles opened across time may be best or at least multiple vintages of the same wine or the same region. Most wines do improve, but some wines and some people seem to get stuck in the infantile phase and like people, wines who never mature are really disappointing jerks.

As wines and humans age, they get more complex; it is as if new layers of knowledge are added upon older ones so that we can speak of mature, aged wines as sort of wise wines, with whom sometimes you have to be patient to receive their wisdom but there is something deep and meaningful in them. At this stage, we begin to give wines human personality traits. We say that some wines are friendly and approachable; others are rather closed and reserved, while still others are dark and moody. We treat them like they belong to different types of social clubs: some wines are graceful, poised, polished, charming, and refined while others are aggressive, disagreeable, unpretentious, and ugly. We bemoan wines that look pretty but have obvious signs of inauthenticity such as additives or severe manipulation—like plastic surgery, it is fine unless we notice it.

We also set up our wines on dates. These dates can be with new palates or with different foods. We speak like Jewish grandmothers proud of their matchmaking abilities when they work—"I just knew she would like the 2005 pinot" or "I just knew that wine would go well with my duck recipe." And when these dates fail, we entertain all the disappointment and second guessing that occur in human relationships.

Sadly, wine can get over the hill. They lose their vivacity and tend to smell more and more like a nursing home. One gets the sense that their best days are behind them. And there is sadness in watching this decline and often regret: I wish I got to spend more time with it at the height of its vivacity. But all things must die and ultimately, wines that are over the hill return to the earth and the cycle of life begins anew.

The ability to form deep relationships with particular wines makes it unique. You might keep sophisticated art or music for extended periods of time, but there is no reciprocity or dynamism in the relationship to a painting or a piece of music. You might be changing over time, but the object of your interest is not. A dish of food may have incredible complexity and be rapidly changing, but you do not experience it over a long duration, usually just for a few hours. Many of the fermented portions of our diet–cheese, coffee, beer, spirits, breads, pickled vegetables, and others—demonstrate complexity and dynamism, but their duration is also limited when compared to wine. As one winemaker told me, "There is no back label with a story on a beer can."

Certain intoxicants, tobacco products, and natural drugs might be consumed over time and display complexity but there is little dynamism present—one does not speak of tobacco getting better over time and no other product places so prominently on it, a birthdate. There may be regional examples that come close to developing a relationship like wine—the Chinese with tea, the Swiss with cheese, the

Japanese with soy sauce, the Italians with balsamic vinegar, the Latin Americans with chilies, Californians with marijuana—but there is no other category where the association is so strong for so long across such a wide array of cultures.

The story of humanity's relationship to wine is unlike any other: humans fall in love with wine like no other non-breathing entity. We fall in love with wine as if it was a person or, perhaps, a deity. The ancient Greeks made wine human through a personality, Dionysius. Perhaps the modern wine devotee is simply doing the same. Dionysius may no longer be invoked, but he is certainly smiling.

Wine as a link to Place

When American romance novelists imagine a debonair French man whose charm sweeps the heroine off her feet, they imagine Jacques Lardière, the silver fox who was for years the wine director at Louis Jadot in Burgundy. Louis Jadot makes everything from the six-dollar Beaujolais to the Burgundy Grand Cru selections for hundreds of dollars a bottle. The latter are stored in a mandala-shaped wine cave, a Buddhist shape that, Lardière informs me, heightens the vibrations that leads to exquisite wines.

On a wet, autumn day in Burgundy, he wanted to prove to me the importance of place in the taste of wine. From barrels, he poured me three Louis Jadot pinots from three vineyards that were adjacent to one another in the Chambertin area of Burgundy. They were all pinot, largely the same clone mixture, farmed largely in the same way, picked around the same time, and vinified in the same manner. Their aromas and tastes could not have been more different. If I didn't know better, I would have thought they were three different varietals. That day Lardière made a convert to the Church of Terroir—a belief that wine is primarily an expression of place.

What is terroir? The most compact and common definition was provided by wine writer Matt Kramer: terroir is "somewhereness." While the term derives from the French word for land or soil, it is everything about the place of origin of a wine that affects the wine: the soil, underlying geology, slope, aspect, and climate. Terroir does not change across vintages, or at least if it changes, the speed is more glacial than fleet. Great wines are a function of the synergy and alignment of four elements: the terroir, the grape variety, the weather that season, and human choices in relation to the first three. Great wines are the "distillation of place" in a bottle,[1] a "translation" of terroir,[2] or even more pithily, "liquid geography," a term that has been so frequently been repeated that it is difficult to provide proper attribution. Great wines, it is argued, reflect their terroir. Terroir becomes intrinsic to their story that we should appreciate.

A bottle of wine reveals a link to its place of origin more than any other product humans make. Indubitably, wine is fundamentally an agricultural product, but it seems better suited than other agricultural products at revealing characteristics specific to particular places. We might say that a cucumber from a specific region has a different character than the same variety grown in a different region or milk from one herd tastes different from milk from another, but wine carries these distinctions to an entirely different level when it speaks of adjacent vineyards producing very different wines from the same variety. In fact, wine is the only agricultural product that puts on every package the specific origin and vintage, nearly without exception. Once cut from the vine, the dead grape becomes a talisman for the place and time of its creation, revealing their imprint when it is vivified by the yeast. I may never have been to Mosel but I've tasted it through its wines. A small slice of blessed earth by a German river screams through its wine, "place matters."

Wines that respect their origin are not products of the earth but expressions of it; they move us out of the tasting room and into a vineyard of a particular time and place. We share in the spirit of a place, if for but a moment. Drinking them is not merely an exercise in thirst quenching but, as Nikos Kazantzakis eloquently states, "communion with the blood of the earth itself." This recognition rips me out of the McWorld that arises so fast and so high around me that it is hard to see there is anything beyond it. It forces me to reconsider myself and my relationship to place and time. The wines that are most true to their origin make us question our own.

The importance of drinking wines that reflect their terroir is not to say that the winemaker is not important. Here the analogy of wine writer Michael Suster is helpful here.[3] He suggests that terroir is like the original composition of a symphony. The conductor and the orchestra do not change the music of Bach or Beethoven, which stays the same over time, but they inevitably interpret it. When we listen to a concert at the New York Philharmonic, we listen for both the underlying masterpiece and the way it has been interpreted by the orchestra. We know some orchestras consistently produce better interpretations of symphonies but even a great orchestra cannot produce something moving from a poor score. Likewise, a poor orchestra can virtually ruin even a masterpiece. So it works with wine. The terroir is more or less constant but each vintage also bears the imprint of the winery and the people making the wine. A great winemaker will make a weak terroir palatable and a great terroir sublime; a lesser winemaker will do neither. Excessive manipulation in the winery can especially hide the voice of the terroir. However, the spiritual winemakers will hold that when a wine is great, it is because the original score handed them was so filled with sublime potential; they just cleverly played the instruments.

The relationship between the grape varietal and terroir has also often been confusing, as some authors seem to make it a constituent element of terroir. However, the grape varietal is more like the focusing agent of terroir than a part of the terroir itself. For winemakers, the grape varietal and clone should provide a clear voice for the underlying terroir. Perhaps the best analogy can be found in the optometrist's office. As anyone who has had their prescription determined knows, one sits in the chair and the optometrist flips through various lenses that each differ slightly to discover which lens provides the clearest focus. The grape varietal act in the same way for the terroir—one can see through a great variety of lenses, but only one or a couple will allow for the greatest degree of precision. This is the varietal that is most at home in a particular terroir.

For example, pinot Noir is the exclusive red grape of Burgundy because generations of trials showed that it best reveals the voice of its unique terroir. One Burgundy producer lamented the challenge of New World winemakers since they do not benefit from centuries of trials; she suspected that the right varietal for many new world locations has yet to be discovered. Paul Draper, of Ridge Wines in Cupertino, told me that when a grape is focusing the vineyard aptly, it is "at home" and this state is apparent in the winery. If one has to work too hard to make a great wine, it is not at home. In the decades of his tenure at Ridge, Draper has tried dozens of vineyard/varietal combinations but rejected most of them after a few years simply because they weren't a great match; the grapes were not at home. Spiritual wine drinkers search for grapes that are at home.

Can the historical culture of a place affect the taste of the wine? Certainly culture affects winemaking traditions of a region and winemaking traditions affects the final taste of the wine, but these shape the humans, not the terroir. Likewise, the aromas of a particular place if they appear in the wine could evoke the place for the drinker. Who does not think of Australia when they have an Australian wine with a bit of Eucalyptus on the nose due to the grapes being planted near the ubiquitous tree of the land down under? This connection to place is really a mental association within the drinker due to the soil, however; the culture itself is not shaping the wine.[4] The interesting point would be if the local culture is directly expressed in the taste of the wine. Some people think it can.

During a year in South Australia, I met with James Erskine, a sommelier turned winemaker who is passionate about wines that speak to the place of their origin. He told me that wines should be drunk ideally in the culture, if not the village, it was created because it would be easier to detect that cultural imprint. When he was responsible for a competition to determine the top 100 wines of South Australia, he commissioned a piece of music that epitomizes South Australia and then played it as the judges were evaluating the wines. The underlying assumption is that a fine wine should taste like its place of origin, or at lease evoke that place in the mind of the drinker.

Burgundy expert Allen Meadows took this link even further in a conversation. Meadows is the critic behind Burghound, the definitive source for pinot around the world. He left his job as Chief Financial Officer of Fidelity National in 1991 to follow his passion to explore pinot full time. Among the earthy Burgundian vignerons (French for, roughly, wine growers), his finely tailored shirt and coiffed hair suggested he still retains a bit of executive in him. His demeanor was also quite business-like, sharing how he can taste 75 wines in a day without compromising his palate and how he monetized his passion for pinot. And yet, when we began to talk about terroir, his Orange County Country Club persona gave way to a mystic hidden within. "The wines of a region do not just evoke the culture and history of their origin," he leaned toward me as if revealing a secret, "they actually carry the energy and spirit of a region." When pressed, he admitted that his idea derives from animism.

The Spirit of Wine

For those whose knowledge of premodern religion is hazy, animism is the notion that everything has a spiritual essence—every tree, every animal, and every rock. Animism is still common in some tribal societies, who often hold more fluid versions of the line between the material and immaterial. For Meadows, a vineyard (at least in Burgundy) has an immaterial spiritual essence that travels with the grape upon picking and lodges itself in the resultant wine. Thus, the most interesting parts of terroir While the wine may bear the spiritual imprint of the place, we need to activate that aspect of our own spiritual receptors to recognize these marks. The soul of wine, for Meadows, is literally the energy or spirit of a land and a people. Drinking wine is to participate with a place, a people, and a stream of history.

While I was initially skeptical of this animistic view of wine, I came to appreciate that drinking a wine that is deeply connected to a place is more than just an encounter with soil, the liquid equivalent of running our hands through the mud. Retsina carries the spirit of Greece, but it has little to do with the soil. Wines that respect their origin also become cultural ambassadors. They link us to people, to traditions, and to stories. We enter into streams of human history and become part of them. Such wines provide a living and vibrant link to the cultural identity of a place. An apocryphal story tells of a man who, fallen on hard times, sold his art collection but kept his wine cellar. When asked why he did not sell his wine, he said, "A man can live without art, but not without culture." For devotees, wine becomes a window into a cultural mindset. If we are sensitive to it, we can come to appreciate through their respective wines the earthiness of the

Burgundian farmer, the ruggedness of the Barrosan immigrant, or crunchy culture of Oregon.

For this reason, wine is intimately tied to the collective identity of places and nations, especially in the Old World. Wine in certain instances has come to be a symbol for the country itself. Hungary's most famous grape is referred to in its national anthem. Ancient Italy was named the "land of vines" by the Greeks. Wine has particularly symbolized France: the French cultural critic Roland Barthes once wrote, "Wine is felt by the French nation to be a possession which is its very own, just like its three hundred and sixty types of cheese and its culture. It is a totem drink."[5] The link to totem is intriguing. A totem is a symbol that both represents the people and contains the spirit of the people. Killing a totem is tantamount to destroying the people. Wine in France plays such a role: in 1872, a French professor declared: "If Burgundy should be wiped out – along with Bordeaux – one could say that France itself had been overthrown."[6]

Recognizing this deep link between a place and wine allows drinkers to travel the globe without ever leaving the glass. If we become sensitive to terroir, we can discover authentic corners of the world reveal the ancient heart of places and people. Unlike the people in the story of the Apostle Paul, we do not have to stand in front of an unknown God. Our oenological deities begin to have stories, but we have to learn them first.

Practical Tips for Contemplating the Story of a Wine

Knowing the biography of a wine, particularly its connection to terroir, takes work for the wine drinker. In part, knowing the full story of the wines you drink is merely a question of research. You need to do your homework. While much of the information about wine is now available online, there are several classic books that most wine devotees will keep within arm's reach which are listed at the end of this chapter.

To discover the story a wine, you might seek to know:

- 🍷 What region, appellation, and vineyard does the wine come from?
- 🍷 What is the soil like of the vineyard?
- 🍷 Where does the varietal or particular clone originate? How did it come to this region?
- 🍷 What is the history of the winery or domaine?
- 🍷 Who are the people who tended the vines or made the wine?
- 🍷 What was the year like during which the grapes developed? Was it dry or wet? Was it warm or cool? Were there climatic events that shaped the growing year?
- 🍷 What was going on when the grapes were picked?

Think of the wine as a sort of time and place capsule, freezing the specifics of its origin until it is opened, perhaps years down the road. The spiritual wine drinker's responsibility is to flesh out the story found within this miraculous act of encoding. Just like a deity or a lover, one comes to appreciate the other more by knowing their story.

Some of the best learning occurs not through studying, but by doing. In fact, the motto of my home university is "Learn by Doing." In the wine environment, a "learn by doing" attitude could take the form of arranging particular tastings that can help you isolate elements of the story of wines. For example, a ladder tasting places the same wine from different years side-by-side. If there is consistency in winemaker and vineyard, such a tasting can provide insights into the impact of the year on the story of the wine. Likewise, a series of different wines from the same producer in the same year, might allow you to recognize the imprint of the winemaker on the wine.

Another fun way to gain the sense of a place is to set up a tasting of multiple wines from the same vineyard, such as Clos du Vugeot in Burgundy or To Kalon in Napa or Bien Nacedo in Santa Barbara or Shae Vineyards in Oregon. As you taste distinct expressions of the vineyard, search for the common denominator to the wines. Are there consistent taste markers, regardless of producer? This is the imprint of terroir.

To engage the life of a wine, you might make a pledge to buy a case of a wine you love and open up one bottle each year for the next twelve years, thus making you witness to the aging process of the wine. Keep notes on each year so that you can relive the transformations over time. If you cannot afford a case, I've learned at least to buy two of every wine so you can watch it evolve over time.

A final warning: in searching for the story of wine, there is a danger here that wine drinking can become such an intellectual exercise that the opportunity for something deeper becomes stymied, not enriched by learning the stories of wines. If one hangs around the world of wine enough, you come across people who can name every first-growth Bordeaux or the soil type of every kilometer of Napa but no longer can really *feel* the wines. The mind must remain a springboard for encounters ultimately beyond the mind and even the body. So, contemplate the story of your wines but don't lose sight of why you study. As all theologians know, the difference between talking about deities and experiencing them is vast. Having one profound encounter even with an "unknown" God is worth more than hundreds of discussions without ever encountering any gods.

Ten Reference Books for a Starter Wine Library:

1. Jancis Robinson, *The Oxford Companion to Wine*
2. Hugh Johnson and Jancis Robinson, *The World Atlas of Wine*
3. Stephen Brooks, *The Complete Bordeaux*
4. Clive Coates, *The Wines of Burgundy*
5. Joseph Bastianich & David Lynch, *Vino Italiano: The Regional Wines of Italy*
6. James Halliday, *James Halliday's Wine Atlas of Australia*
7. Warren Moran, *New Zealand Wine: The Land, The Vines, The People*
8. Jon Bonne, *The New California Wine: A Guide to the Producers and Wines Behind a Revolution in Taste*
9. Dieter Braatz, Ulrich Sautter, & Ingo Swoboda, *Wine Atlas of Germany*
10. Evan Goldstein, *Wines of South America: The Essential Guide*

Becoming a Wine Devotee
Step 2: Mindfulness and the Art of Wine Drinking

In the middle of winter, a select group of women in ancient Greece would climb the 8000-foot peak of Mt. Parnassus. They were called the *maenads,* the mad ones, because they ran naked, danced wildly, played with snakes, and beat the ground with a sacred rod. The women reportedly captured a wild animal, tore it to pieces, and then ate it raw. Some say it wasn't an animal but an infant. They were trying to coax the god Dionysius from the dead, to raise him up, so that there would be fruit the next year and wine to share. Dionysius had to be seduced or there would be no harvest. Yet, the secret was that Dionysius wanted to be seduced; it was through own his power that these women seduced him. The mad ones were merely embodying the Dionysian spirit. The God of Wine dwelled within them; he was who made them mad in the first place.

The extraordinary and beautiful aspect of wine is its ability to connect the drinker to times past, far off lands, and the earth that we all share. For a connection to occur, however, both sides of the equation need to be fully present. Just as you wouldn't serve an ice-cold Bordeaux, so drinkers with the wrong attitude will preclude the possibility of having a meaningful experience with wine. It does not matter if a 1945 Petrus is in front of someone if that person is distracted, unreceptive, or otherwise mistuned to oenological glory. Wines may transmit messages but the drinker must be in a state to receive them. We need to be filled with the Dionysian spirit, perhaps without the naked dancing and infanticide.

Jacque Ladierre, the former winemaker at Burgundy's Louis Jadot and a fervent practitioner of Buddhist meditation, conveyed a similar lesson that he attributed to his practice of Buddhism. He argues that the transcendent wine experiences are akin to spiritual meditation: unlike other alcohols that tend to dull the mind, fine wine clears it; it "washes the mental world," in his words. With such clarity, we are able to detect higher levels of vibration. What are vibrations? For him, it is the zest of life. It is the energy of the universe that suffuses all things, but exists in some places more than others. Burgundy is particularly full of vibrations and, of course, pinot is the ideal grape for transmitting them, but all great wines contain and inspire higher levels of vibration. Some of his own wines are stored in a cellar the shape of mandala, which he claims is ideal for bolstering the vibrations.

The Spirit of Wine

Ladierre argues that these vibrations are physical but they are undetectable, at least with current technology, but mindful humans can still sense them. When humans are open to these vibrations, they act like "Jacob's ladder." He explains, "you discover that you are more than you are." This occurs not only because you take in the vibrations contained in the wine but because the process opens you up (or perhaps attunes you) to recognize the vibrations all around. The experience with wine offers the drinker new planes of existence, operating on higher levels of vibration. As importantly, drinking wine in this way becomes a sacred form of meditation. Once news of this spiritual practice spreads, the monasteries may never be the same again.

The wine drinker must learn to be aware of these vibrations. Some might call this the Dao, but the notion is straight-forward: there exists just below the surface an energizing current in life that something in our everyday existence keeps us from. There are various ways to access this current—music, sports, religion, etc… Transcendent wine is just one avenue to place us in touch with it. The person drinking the right kind of wine in the right kind of mental state with the right kind of people is like the musician channeling the muses or the athlete hitting her stride. A transcendent wine experience is merely a peak performance in another field.

While the idea of a non-physical current undergirding the universe sounds religious, it is not necessarily so. Psychologist Mihaly Csikszentmihalyi has made a career of studying flow after observing that some artists seem to enter into phases where they lose a sense of the outer world and act as if they are channeling some outside muse. He argued in his most popular book, simply titled *Flow,* that certain activities create this feeling of flow. These sorts of activities require a sense of continual discovery driven by increasingly complex formulations. When we give our all to such an environment, something switches in our brain. We feel swept away from our everyday surroundings and schedules; our concern for the self disappears yet we have a strong sense of being directed towards a goal; we feel energized and joyous; in short, we feel like we are in the flow rather than fighting against it. We are in the groove rather than grating against it. The gateway to such wine *flow* is learning to be mindful, one of the greatest gifts of Zen Buddhism to the world.

Zen and the Art of Wine Drinking

A legend from China says that the renowned Buddhist monk who introduced Zen to East Asia, Bodhidharma, was in the habit of falling asleep during his daily meditations. One day, infuriated by his inability to stay awake, Bodhidharma cut off his eyelids and tossed them out the window. His eyelids, however, nourished the soil and grew into the first tea plants in Asia. Ever since, Asian culture has been intimately tied to tea as much as France has been tied to wine. In the last decades, Asia has developed a wine palate, and an expensive one at that, but their relationship with tea may just reveal one of the keys to making wine spiritual in your life.

In Japan, preparing and serving tea has become a religious rite. Chado—the Way of Tea—requires as much discipline as any martial art. In the ceremony, a woman (and it is usually a woman today) slowly, deliberately, and gracefully makes tea through a series of predefined movements. While sometimes there are special venues for the ceremony, it really is less about consecrating a place as it is about developing a mindset. The precise steps differ by school, region, and even time of year, but the general process is the same: after some preparation, a bell summons the guests to the ceremonial area where they are greeted by the host and exchange bows. The host then purifies the ritual utensils—the bowl, caddy, scoop, and whisk—which are treated with care and reverence. With a clear mind and composed state, the host then meticulously prepares the tea; there is no rush as the daily drive toward efficiency and production for which the Japanese are famous has no place in the Way of Tea. When the tea is ready, the host bows to each guest and they all partake of the same bowl with due sobriety for a sacred event. A second cup of tea and some sweets may follow and there is a period for more casual conversation. The defining ethos is *ichigo ichie*: one time, one meeting; that is, being present at this event, this moment, with these people. The ceremony ends with the host bowing from the door to honor her guests and then Tea time is over.

While the practice of the Way of Tea is external, it is meant to transform the inside of the practitioner. The roots of the ceremony come from Zen Buddhism, in which mindfulness of the present is a central religious goal. The goal is be fully *here, now*. Humans have a tendency, Zen says, of being anywhere other than the present: we live in the past as we think about the things we do or the changes we should have made; we live in the future as we hope and plan for a better tomorrow; we live in fantasy or cyberspace, places that lack concrete reality; we want to be anywhere but where we are.

The path to Enlightenment in Zen begins when we can learn to be still, present, and aware. Chado is an exercise in awareness cultivation. It extracts you from the rush of the day, slows you down, and makes you pay attention to what is before your eyes. It aims to unify our balkanized selves; to make us whole and aware again. It is a tea ceremony that is ultimately not about drinking tea. It is a way of training the mind and opening the heart that results in inner serenity and, perhaps, enlightenment.

Spiritual wine drinkers need to cultivate a Chado of Wine: a way of drinking wine that induces mindfulness of the present. I've come to see the rituals connected with wine as the vehicles of mindfulness. For example, the laborious process of pulling a cork can become a marker to settle the mind. As one wine devotee told me, "It doesn't matter how frantic my day has been or how many plates I am spinning. When I come home, I go to my designated spot, pick out my bottle of wine, slowly put the corkscrew in and by the time the cork is out and I am tasting the wine, it is as if I entered another world." The corkscrew becomes a slow tool of inner transformation. Of course, there are wine rabbits and screw caps that quicken the process, but those in the wine world cherish their corkscrews not out of nostalgia but for the mindfulness they induce.

Decanting a wine can also settle the mind. You cannot rush the decanting process. It is deliberate, like the making of tea in Chado. Eventually the wine is poured—slowly again, for too much vigor into a wine glass will just lead to being spilled. The wine is then sniffed, another process that cannot be rushed. Finally, the wine is not gulped down but sipped, deliberately and with attention.[1] Good wine begs you to pay attention to it, drawing your mind away from wherever it was

134

and demanding your full attention. All these rituals—the cork, the decanting, the pouring, the sniffing, the sipping—these are all life-decelerators. Just like with Chado, this process makes you stop and pay attention—be present with yourself and with your chosen vehicle to go beyond yourself, wine. One bottle. One moment. One sip.

Practical Tips on Cultivating Wine Mindfulness

1. Free Yourself From Expectation and Judgement.

In part, cultivating such mindfulness in drinking entails an attitude of openness to authentically experience the wine, however it is found. So often, those who have been wine connoisseurs for a while instantly move to judgment, for everyone wants to be a critic. Instead of experiencing the wine fully, they compare it to other wines they've drunk, calibrate it to some imagined ideal of the varietal, and compose in their head a witty tasting note to post on their blog. Expectations are particularly noxious to profound wine experiences. Instead of establishing preconceived notions of what the wine *should* taste like, meet the wine where it is at that particular moment. Prepare to be surprised. Be present. Allow the wine to lead you. Withhold judgment until it has had time to seduce you properly. Become vulnerable to the wine and see what it has to offer.

2. Set an environment conducive to appreciating the wine

Tossing down some industrial wine beverage over a Big Mac will not be a spiritual experience for most people. It is not just that industrial wines rarely produce transcendent experiences—though it is probably true—but it is also that spiritual wine experiences require a degree of mindfulness that is incommensurate with the fast food environment.

The surrounding environment can also be critical to encouraging mindfulness. Just as the religious environments for worship or meditation differ remarkably, here there is no simple formula. For some people, a silent and still environment may allow the person to isolate his or her response to the wine; for others, music and candlelight could enhance the powers of perception; still others might want discussion and dialogue to unravel the mysteries they encounter. The point is that using wine spiritually requires a degree of self-awareness as to what kind of environment is most conducive to encouraging mindfulness.

3. Have a wine routine that you follow

Having a routine can be helpful in establishing the right mind frame. Just as basketball players might approach their free throws with the same pattern of actions every time, so the wine drinker may choose to ritualize their wine experience. Think of the following list as a suggestion, rather than a dogmatic catechism:

- **See**. Take time to really look at the wine. Hold it up to the light. Observe the color and the shifts of the color across the spectrum as one approaches the edge of the glass. Ascertain its degree of brilliance and clarity.
- **Swirl** the wine in the glass, giving it oxygen and releasing its aromas. There are scientific reasons behind this stage but there are also ritual elements to it. It can become a physical cue to center oneself before the encounter moves to the next stage.
- **Smell**. A large glass helps to capture the aromas and allow you to place your nose all the way in it. I often

close my eyes here and occasionally plug an ear to isolate the sense of smell. This step is also an exercise in smell memory, which is often challenging. Where did you smell something similar? What feelings are the smells evincing?

- **Sip** the wine. Here is the most central act of drinking but the point is to allow the wine to coat the entire inside of your mouth. Move it around all areas of your mouth. Explore not just the taste but the texture. Observe how your mouth reacts to it.
- **Swallow** or **spit**. New sensations arise when you swallow the wine. Here is when you gauge the length of the wine. At what stage does its presence make itself felt most strongly? Does it linger like an old friend or leave a bad taste in your mouth, literally?
- **Savor**. Now is the time for reflection and contemplation. Be present not just for how you expected to react to the wine or how you are supposed to react to the wine, but how did you actually feel? Were there times, especially in your life outside of wine, that you felt something similar? What is your gut reaction to the wine?
- **Share**. The six stages above are a gradual process of interiorization whereby the wine moves from external subject to a deep source of internal contemplation. This final step begins to reverse the process. You are asked to articulate the experience to others. As we will see in the section below, you should not be constrained by the traditional or industry-approved modes of description. However,

here is the opportunity to come to terms, quite
literally, with the wine just experienced.
The seven S-es are a helpful rubric for remembering to
remain mindful during the wine drinking process.
Undoubtedly there are many others and no shortage of books
to enhance your wine appreciation skills, but the point here is
that having a wine tasting routine can serve as a tool to
remain mindful throughout the process.

4. Slow Down

Appreciating wine is not a race. Even if there is a larger
process of comparison going on in a wine tasting, allow each
wine to speak to you before moving on. Savor it. Appreciate
it. The seven S-es of wine tasting should not be seen as a
checklist that you celebrate its speedy conclusion but rather as
a sort of muscle-memory of deliberate slowing down. They
remind you to stop and appreciate every aspect of tasting the
wine, before moving on to another aspect.

The Philosopher Immanuel Kant argued that human ethics
comes down to treating each person as an end in itself rather
than a means to some other goal. Likewise, a spiritual wine
drinker treats each wine as an end in itself, with a message
that is worthy of listening to on its own terms. This ethical
mandate calls us to stop and give the wine our attention.
Before moving onto the next wine in the sequence, slow
down and appreciate the wine before you in gratitude.

5. Cultivate Gratitude

Remember, the wine has spent sometimes years becoming,
evolving, and maturing before it presents itself to you.
Acknowledging this effort means cultivating an appreciation

for the wine as it is. This process does not have to mean vocally thanking the wine or bowing before it, but rather can just be an internal recognition of all the elements that contributed to giving you this experience: the earth that provided the nutrients for the vines; the vines and sun that together created the grapes; the people who picked the grapes; the winemaker who oversaw the grapes transformation into wine; the wine staff that bottled the wine, shared its story with you, and often carried it to you; your host, who provided the environment for this wine to be drunk. Even if the drinking experience is far from transcendent, recognizing the contributions of all the factors that led to this moment of drinking should elicit feelings of gratitude within the spiritual wine drinker. The world has conspired to give you this moment, this glass, and these people to share it with. Give thanks.

Becoming a Wine Devotee: Step 3: Appreciate the Mystery of Wine

The sign that you've made it in the historical Jewish scholarship is when your name is employed so often that you are bestowed an acronym for ease: Rambam, Ramban, Rama, Rashba, and Ritva are all famous historical rabbis whose teachings still percolate around the halls of Yeshivas, Rabbinical colleges. The most famous Rabbinical biblical commentator of all time, however, is Rashi, or more properly Rabenu Shlomo Yitzchaki. In the 11th century, Rashi wrote the most important commentaries on the Torah and Talmud, the two most holy books in Judaism. In 1475, his commentary on the books of Moses became the first book ever printed in Hebrew and since the 16th century, no print edition of the Talmud has appeared without his commentary on every page. Today, he is simply known as the "teacher of Israel." Not bad for a man who earned his keep not by being a rabbi but by making and selling wine.[1]

Rashi was born and spent most of his productive years in Troyes, which is in the Champagne region of France. His dad was a vigneron and Rashi himself provides clues to his life in wine. In one letter he apologizes for the short response but, he explains, he was in the middle of vintage; in another letter, he begs for forgiveness if he seems distracted but he was filling wine barrels that elsewhere he mentions were engraved with his own name. He compares good opinions to the "best wines"[2] and his commentary has been called the "wine of torah."[3] For Rashi, wine is an opening into the mysteries of God and creation. Rashi tells us that this insight is the point of the story of Noah.

Noah is usually credited as being the world's first winemaker. Charged with the simple task of reestablishing every living thing on earth, Noah comes off the ark, plants a vineyard, and proceeds to get drunk, which doesn't end well.[4] The decision to first plant a vineyard or at least get tipsy with wine after an epic journey like his probably seems quite reasonable to most readers of this book, but Jewish commentators have long wondered why Noah began the "humanity 2.0 project" with a wine binge. An intriguing hypothesis is offered by Rabbi Meir, a second-century Rabbinic sage: he argued that the Tree of Knowledge from the garden of Eden was actually a grape vine.[5] Thus, humanity was initially led astray due to Adam's wine drinking.[6] Noah's choice to plant a vineyard was then motivated by a hope to redeem the fruit of the vine but, despite his good intentions, he only perpetuated the curse by allowing himself to get drunk.[7]

Such a precarious connection between the thirst for wine and the thirst for intimate knowledge of God is found in numerous Jewish writers. The Talmud, a collection of sayings and interpretation by the Rabbinic sages of the early centuries of the common era, contains the following enigmatic statement about wine: "Anyone who retains a clear mind with wine has the knowledge of his Creator ... he rivals the knowledge of the Seventy Elders, for wine was given with letters equaling 70 as is the mystery of the Torah—when wine goes in, secrets go out."[8]

As suggested by the statement, one might need to pour oneself a glass of wine, for I am about to reveal the secret of this passage. The "Seventy Elders" is symbolic for the wisest of all knowledge of God for it represents the sanhedrin of seventy elders through whom the wisdom of Moses and all the prophets were passed. The numerical value of 70 attached to wine requires one to understand the system of *gematria*. In the ancient Hebrew, consonant letters were given numerical equivalents so one could "add up" a word to reach a numerical value. In this case, the Hebrew word for wine, *yayin*, is comprised of three Hebrew letters: yod (10) + yod (10) + nun (50) = 70. The Talmudic passage points out that this happens to be the same numerical value of the Hebrew word for mystery, *sod* (sameh (60) + vav (6) + daled (4) = 70). Thus the passage suggests that as one consumes wine, the mystery of God is revealed to people.

Adam and Noah were right after all, even if their execution was a bit sloppy (drunk). In fact, elsewhere in the Talmud, wine is said to open the heart to reason[9] and one who possesses all of God's knowledge is referred to as an *eshkolos*, a full grape cluster.[10] A later commentator argues that the wisdom of God and wine are one in the same.[11] And the reward for gaining the "Fifty Gates of Understanding" in the Talmud is "wine guarded in its grapes since the six days of Creation."[12] It seems all the mysteries of the universe can be discovered at the bottom of a glass. Or at least so I hope to believe.

Those on the path of spirituality of wine learn to appreciate the mysteries of the universe through wine. Spiritual wine drinkers discover in wine a window into the unseen and a harbinger of hope for a deeper existence. This chapter explores this step in the wine journey.

The Modern Need for Mystery

In a speech in 1917, one of the founders of sociology, Max Weber, argued that humanity had entered into a new epoch that he called "de-mystification," the elimination of mystery. He did not think that everything had been explained, but rather that we now believed that everything was explainable. Magical and spiritual effects had been replaced by systematic, logical, and verifiable processes. Providence had shifted away from deities and toward science; faith and trust had shifted from heaven to earth. "The fate of our world is characterized," Weber writes, "above all, by the 'disenchantment of the world'."

The change in mental camps is most apparent when one considers the faculty of wonder: the pre-industrialized world did not have to cultivate wonder; it was a part of who they were. The sun regularly coming up each morning, the renewal of vegetation each spring, and the rising dough were all greeted with awe and wonderment, as was nearly everything else. Wonderment has fallen on tough times today. Even children in school are tested on facts, not their ability to wonder. Some of the only areas of true mystery left are the pricing of airline tickets and the specific date when an expectant mother will give birth (and even the latter is quickly falling aside with the rise of scheduled caesarians). To allow something to remain mysterious is seen as a sin against science. Modernity may not have removed all mystery yet, but it will, or so the logic of the modern world depends.

For some people, this mechanized and rational world offers a sense of security, especially if the alternative is sheer randomness. However, the scientific fundamentalism behind the demystification of the world has been incongruent with people's experiences and left people feeling empty. They want to preserve the place of mystery in human experience and return to a place of humility before the world. Perhaps ironically, this movement has been driven in part by scientists such as theoretical physicists and deep-space astronomers whose scientific discoveries have led them to awe and wonder. However, the artists, poets, and musicians have always been the primary portals to mystery. "The answer is never the answer," author Ken Kesey pleads, "What's really interesting is the mystery…to seek mystery, evoke mystery, plant a garden in which strange plants grow and mysteries bloom." The search for precisely such a garden has led to the fruit of the vine and the mysterious properties of wine.

For those seeking a spiritual relationship to wine, the fruit of the vine can provide a recurring source of mystery. This mystery begins with the vineyard itself. Science has been helpful in explaining the link between vineyards and great wine but the secret behind the magic of legendary vineyards such as Romanée-Conti , To Kalon, or Hill of Grace tilts toward the mysterious. Most reflective people in the wine industry accept that the *terroir* of a place translates into the grapes, but this process is shrouded in mystery that eludes scientific testing. The mystery only deepens as the cycles of the vine work their way through the year. The modern viticulturist can turn the soil into a laboratory filled with chemicals and devoid of predators; employ copious soil meters; use a variety genetically engineered for resilience; precisely control the water and shade; and yet, the agricultural process is still grounded in the foundational Eleusinian mystery of death and rebirth, Demeter and Persephone. As nearly every winemaker will bemoan, no computer or scientific logarithm can even accurately predict the weather or the way particular meteorological conditions affect the grapes. No robot can or will reproduce the quality that comes out of the human engagement with Clos de Vougeot or Montrachet. Mystery is inherent to viticulture.

Perhaps the greatest source of mystery comes once the grapes are picked and fermentation begins. To watch a batch of wine ferment is to watch a miracle unfold. Even if we understand the molecular science behind it, one gets the sense that the mystery behind the formation of all life is being witnessed. In Chaucer's England, yeast was known as "godisgoode," for it was one of the clearest reflections of grace in all the earth. The American Founding Father Ben Franklin was in awe of the process: "We hear of….[the Christian tradition] of turning water in to wine as a miracle. But this conversion is, through the goodness of God, made every day before our eyes. Behold the rain which descends from heaven upon our vineyards, and which incorporates

146

itself with the grapes to be changed into wine; a constant proof that God loves us and wants us to be happy." Temperature-controlled tanks and spinning cones can mask this miracle but the very inception of wine is intricately connected with the mystery of life formation. It is like watching the first lines of Genesis play out each vintage.

The mystery continues when the wine eventually arrives in the hands of the consumer. We get a sort of hazy glance through the green bottle that can give us some tantalizing clues (is it clear or does it have sediment? it is dark or light?), but we don't really know what we are going to experience. This mystery runs deeper than just a function of deliberate concealment, the effect of keeping ourselves from experiencing it. It is actually something structural in the periodic nature of our relationship with wine: just as I will not know a wine's future, I also do not know its past. *Who* it is will always be elusive to me. If I am so lucky, today I may be able to have a 1947 Château Petrus but I will never have it like it was in 1947, 1957, 1967, or any year after or in between. I may hear of others' experiences with it and I may detect some of its history once I taste it, but some portion of it will remain forever elusive. As a result, I may love a wine, but I will never fully know it.

Once we open it, the sign of a great wine is the wonder it produces. "Great wines don't make statements, they pose questions," British wine writer Hugh Johnson is fond of saying, but the portion missing from this observation is that the answers to these questions are not readily available. Great wines surprise us and then we struggle with them and engage their mystery. No matter how many sensory evaluation classes we may have taken, great wines draw us in and leave us speechless, as Terry Theise eloquently captures:

> The greatest wines are the ones you can't write notes about because you're weeping, overcome with their loveliness. This happened to me in a restaurant in Paris one evening; the waiter must have thought my wife had just told me she didn't love me anymore and was absconding with the plumber. Nah, it was just the damned Jurancon. This, like all wine experiences, will jump out of the darkness at you, but it's okay, it's part of the spell. Don't fear the weeper.

We search for descriptors like the mystic searches for words to describe the encounter with God—the better the wine, the harder it is to describe. Great wines take us by the hand to places of wonderment and then don't let go of their grasp. In fact as the wine opens over the course of the evening or week, it continues to lead us to new and often unexpected places. We can decant it, fill the remainder of a bottle with nitrogen, or see what kind of wonderment awaits pairing with certain foods, but we are pretty much just along for the ride: the wine is fulfilling its own destiny for its encounter with oxygen. We just witness and experience the spectacle.

The wine collector has a special relationship to mystery. Even if one is intimately familiar with a wine, every tasting will be different on a number of different levels. To begin with, bottle variation exists naturally. Even if from the same batch (genetically identical we might say), wine tends to vary across a case, especially if enclosed by cork or made with limited sulfites. Wine is also, however, a living entity or more precisely, a living entity in the midst of dying. All wine is

148

somewhere on the path to vinegar and every time we approach the wine, it will be at a different stage on that slow march toward death.

Wine drinkers are also always changing, not only physically (our palates change as we age, for example) but also mentally and emotionally. We might be in a different emotional state or intellectual state since the last time we tasted the wine. At the very least, the consumer is a more experienced wine drinker than the last time a wine was approached. Furthermore, the environment such as the food pairings, the music, and the company is going to be different. In sum, the wine, the drinker, and the environment are always shifting, making every tasting totally unique: it will never be or can be predicted or duplicated. If this is so, tasting the same wine over multiple years or vintages is to enter into the unknown. A cellar can become a den of mystery.

If so, the wine cellar offers a particularly benevolent encounter with mystery. At one level, any collection such as coins, stamps, or beanie babies is premised on a belief that it will provide future pleasure. The difference with a wine collection, however, is that each bottle is not just potential for intellectual and emotional enjoyment, but also a sensual pleasure that improves with age. Only certain kinds of cigars, tea, and spirits play this sort of role and then only weakly. Yet, the specific character of future enjoyment is *unknown*— some of the bottles will disappoint while others will turn out to be pleasant surprises and staring at them, no one can know for sure. This uncertainty is the mystery driving the system. We are always waiting of the next epiphany and we are willing to suffer through considerable lesser wines in order to discover it.

The challenge is that wine devotees cannot predict when we are going to have such an epiphany wine. They *know* that it is possible. They *hope* that it will be the next bottle. If it is not this bottle, there is always hope for the next cellared bottle, the next vintage, or the next winery. Cellared wine is bottled hope. Wine thus provides an unusually safe environment for people to allow mystery to re-enter their lives since the playing field of mystery is tilted decidedly toward the positive. It is as if every bottle is a mystery with potential for heaven or a better rebirth with only minimal fear of damnation or devaluation. It is no wonder that people find it appealing.

The skill of the wine devotee is to be aware of the mystery and allow themselves to dwell in it. In the "Drops of God," the protagonist has a ritual when he moves from the physical characteristics of wine to its deeper level: Shizuku says, "Awaken, Bacchus." Although not all wine devotees will say this out loud, the sentiment is repeated throughout the wine world. When wine devotees close their eyes and maybe lose themselves in silence or stirring music, they allow themselves to move beyond the demystified modern world and into a mysterious world made possibly by the magical touch of Bacchus.

Wine as a link to Transcendence

"God is dead….And we have killed him." Nietzsche proclaimed this famous statement in the 19th century. He was probably premature by about a hundred years, but his insight aptly captures an important development of the modern world: he did not mean (as it is widely assumed) that there is no God but rather that humans no longer act as if God exists. We killed God, by living without any sense of transcendence in our lives.

For Nietzsche, the death of God was a good thing but in the 1960s, the great Religious Studies scholar Mircea Eliade sought to reverse this trend. He demonstrated in his writings that archaic peoples had a continual link to the transcendent; they were always living under heaven or the Dao, the Dreaming, or whichever phrase they used to symbolize the sacred. Their lives reveal that humans naturally align themselves with the sacred and are most real when dwelling within Transcendence. Only modern, industrialized peoples deliberately obscure these connections as we compact the multi-layered universe into a single story. Transcendence was now something that had to be deliberately sought out. For those on the path of making wine spiritual, wine can become vehicles of transcendence.

Something magical occurs when you sip a great bottle of wine that is difficult to capture in prose. Galileo Gallilei evokes the feelings that arise when he proclaimed, "Wine is sunlight, held together by water!" Like listening to great musical compositions or standing before a spire in a great cathedral, the encounter with great wine leads us to look beyond the terrestrial plane. The make us believe in, as Matt Kramer found with pinot, "a Presence in the universe beyond our own."[13] This is part of the draw of the epiphany moment that led so many into a lifetime passion with wine: it was an awakening of the transcendent receptors within us after a long slumber. It is the lightening of a spiritual flame that we may have forgotten exists. Such experiences may be rare, but an encounter with such a wine opens our dormant spiritual eyes and then dilates them. They resurrect God from modernity's trash heap.

It changes the course of lives, sometimes in dramatic ways. Even if one wanted, one could not forget it. Anglo-French writer Hilaire Belloc captures this sentiment in his famous line: "When that this too, too solid flesh shall melt, and I am called before my Heavenly Father, I shall say to him Sir, I don't remember the name of the village, and I don't remember the name of the girl, but the wine was Chambertin." The context of this confession is perhaps unimportant but it is the long ago experience with a wine that he anticipates carrying into the next world. The ability of wine to form such deep grooves is in part the point of Jonathan Nossiter's evocative insight: "Wine is memory in its most liquid and dynamic form."[14] We remember these moments so strongly because they are tucked away in an altogether different recess of the mind than ordinary knowledge and experience. It is as if we have a cavity waiting to be filled with extraordinary experiences that lift us up beyond the material. In the past, these experiences happened most often with rosaries or mala beads in hand. Today, a wine glass might just take their place.

Practical Tips for Appreciating the Mystery of Wine

1. Taste Blind, Deaf, and Dumb

Marketers of wine, like most capitalists, are masters of manipulation. They use the name, label, and story of their wine to sell imaginary worlds that they hope you will want to inhabit: a regal-looking traditional label transmits a message that comes with Cadillacs and the estates of Napa or Bordeaux. By contrast, a tweety-bird label suggests something fun and frivolous while a good wine pun (such as Randall Graham's classic "A Critique of Pure Riesling") announces erudition and sophistication amidst the fun. The goal of marketers is to frame your experience with the wine. However, on the spiritual path of wine, you sometimes need to be liberated from their coercive goals. A spiritual experience might just happen when you are open to whatever mystery the wine wants to offer.

For me, being open to the wine itself requires that I occasionally taste blind, deaf, and dumb. That is, I drink wines without input from the outside world. I appreciate it, I shut down all the extraneous senses: I will close my eyes, plug my ears, and just allow the wine to wash over my palate to see what it evokes. Isolating myself to the exterior world seems to open my inner world to the mystery of wine. In this way, it becomes a raw tasting experience without the prejudgment of others. If there is mystery to be found, it seems easier to discover it without the outside world intruding.

2. Taste at Extraordinary Places

Not all places seem to be created spiritually equal. Some places seem to have a great power to them, that we sometimes even feel physically. Think of the Oracle at Delphi in Greece, or the Temple in Jerusalem where the presence of God resided for the Jews, or Luxor in Egypt, or even natural Cathedrals such as Yosemite or Uluru (Ayer's Rock). These places make you sense the sacred in a way that is far more difficult in Bakersfield, the Bronx, or Brisbane.

Historically, some people have even held that the spiritual, physical, and psychic energies in the earth form a sort of grid or a series of veins and arteries in the earth. There are lines of energy or power that if you are aware, you will sense but just like if you don't have a compass, you won't be aware of the magnetic properties of earth, so if you are not attuned to these energies, you might not even notice them. These are sometimes called Ley lines or dragon lines, but the basic idea is that there is a matrix of cosmic energy that creates a grid where some points these energies converge into particularly powerful places. These are places of great wonder, great spiritual insight, and great healing. Some of these are long known: the pyramids in Egypt, the monoliths at Stonehenge and Glastonbury, Easter Island of South America, Jerusalem, Varanasi in India, Angkor Wat in Cambodia, Macchu Picchu in Peru—the idea here is that the ancient people did not randomly choose to make their sacred centers here rather than there. Rather, they were attuned to the energies better than we are. And so the world is full of these places of convergence, or earth chakras, or cosmic vortexes.

Drinking wine at one of these places can often create a memorable experience. Once I led a group in a wine tasting at the Temple of Poseidon at Cape Sounion near Athens, Greece. As the sun was setting through the ancient Doric columns, the rather prosaic wines of rural Greece drunk in plastic glasses tasted nothing short of magical. Having tasted many of these same wines previously in stores and restaurants, the wines tasted different at this site, with these people, at that particular moment. Some wines beg to be heard but it takes the spiritual energy of a unique place to amplify their message. Sometimes wines can channel the spiritual energy of a place.

So bring local wines to these places of spiritual convergence. Be open to the mysteries that await.

3. Hide some wines away

Wine Spectator, the influential wine magazine from America, always has some images near the back of the magazine that depict usually a celebrity's wine cellar. With magnificent cellars filled with rare wines, it is wine porn for the average wine collector. Indeed, most wine enthusiasts dream of having a cellar worthy of Wine Spectator, but in reality have wine cellars that are considerably more modest. With the advent of online tracking of wine, it is easier than ever to keep our wines organized, creating lists of our wines by drink by dates or meal pairing. While I appreciate the value of such wine regimentation, sometimes discovering a long-forgotten wine in a hidden location can create a transcendent wine experience.

When you store an occasional case of wines under an interior stairway or in the crawl space, you have the chance to discover something new that might just blow you away. "Forget" some wine at a vacation house, a child or parents' house, or in a friends' cellar. The point is to create moments in your wine life where the expectation game—drink this wine with this score at this time—is denuded of its influence over you. Sometimes the unexpected "discovery" of a wine will lead to surprising insights.

4. Let Wines Choose You

From a family of barristers and fresh out of Oxford, Jasper Morris followed his nose to Burgundy in 1979 and spent a lifetime tasting and selling some of the greatest of the century. His magnum opus on Burgundy, called *Inside Burgundy,* provides personal details on over 1000 vineyards in the region (as well as dozens of sexual scandals among their producers). When I interviewed him in his country manor in rural Burgundy, he still conveyed the infectious enthusiasm for Burgundy as when he arrived forty years prior with his signature unruly mop of reddish hair which has now thinned. When I asked him about the greatest wines he has drunk in his career, he shifted the conversation, leaning forward as if to share some wisdom with me, the Burgundian neophyte: "The best wines have not been at the famous tastings or celebrated dinners, but when my wife and I are alone, on a rainy afternoon in Burgundy, and we go down to the cellar and let the wines choose us."

Jasper later explained that picking the right wine for the occasion is less an arithmetic formula of the mind and more an intuitive act of the heart. He encouraged me to stand before a rack of wine and sense which wine *feels* right for the moment. You don't need a special occasion to open your most coveted wines; rather, sometimes you just need a moment that feels right. Turn off the analytic mind and be open to listening to the wines themselves. Such an attitude awakens the wine drinker to wonder because it quells the instinct to be a critic and fosters a wine tasting environment shaped instead by the heart and soul.

I have to admit that since hearing Jasper's advice, sometimes the voices of the wine in my collection seem stubbornly silent. Yet, there is also something liberating about Jasper's method: you don't have the save the greatest wines for the most important markers in life. Sometimes a quiet Thursday afternoon with someone you love is the best time to open your best wine. Don't feel compelled to save your wines for big birthdays, weddings, and anniversaries. Sometimes the best wine experiences come when you least expect them.

There is also perhaps a deeper lesson: moments of oenological wonder sometimes need to be seized, not planned. Follow your wine bliss. Carpe vinum.

5. Free Yourself from Wine Rubrics

In ancient Greek physiology, there existed an intermediary organ that stood between your sense perceptions and your mind. Called the *nous*, it acted as a sort of filter that shaped how our raw experiences of this world are presented to our brains. Psychological and spiritual challenges were seen fundamentally as issues of a malfunctioning *nous*. Those who modern psychologists would classify as schizophrenics or even psychopaths would be seen as having misaligned nous-es that did not allow them to see the world as it actually was. Yet, while schizophrenics and psychopaths may represent the extreme, most philosophers held that we all have dysfunctional nous-es to some degree. For early Christians, the sinful character of humans was explained by the fall of humans with Adam and Eve, which resulted in a darkened and misguided nous for all of humanity. The mark of a Christian then was a nous polished and sharpened by Christ. The Apostle Paul writes, "Do not be conformed to this world, but be transformed by the renewal of your *nous.*" (Romans 12:2) Salvation means to see the world through the filter of God.

Modern physiology no longer includes a *nous*, but we still hold that our past experiences and genetic vicissitudes have led to frames by which we process our experiences. Some of these frames present altered realities, such as when we interpret the compliment of a spouse as a secret criticism. Much of modern psychology is rooted in guiding clients to reframe their interpretation of their reality.

The world of wine is infused with standardized frames that shape our encounters with wine. These are the rubrics that tell us to look for fruit, acids, color, tannin, oak levels, and other common metrics when evaluating wines. As described in chapter two's discussion of Ann Nobel's aroma wheel, these rubrics have often been codified and dogmatically indoctrinated in young wine professionals. Yet, even if one is not tasting wines for a living, these rubrics often will become second nature to us. When we approach new wines, many of us have a mental check list of qualities and characteristics that we look for. In other words, we have a wine *nous* that filters our raw experience with the wine.

As an analytic tool, such a mental wine frame can be useful as one learns to hone your tastes in wine. This analytic process allows us to move from "I just like that wine" to "I like high acid, unoaked, low tannin Rhone wines from cool climates." However, such a metric often impedes the cultivation of a sense of wonder. Our minds are so busy analyzing and categorizing that there is not enough room for the heart and soul to make their way into our wine experience. Wonder might start in the mind but it has to transcend it. So letting go of the rubrics from time to time is an essential quality in cultivating wonder in your spiritual journey into wine. Change gears and allow yourself just to appreciate a wine experience freed from the shackles of a critical lens. To paraphrase the Apostle Paul, "Do not be conformed to the ways of the wine world, but be transformed by a renewal of your wine *nous*." Seek merely to be with the wine and all things will be added unto you. Om.

Becoming a Wine Devotee: Step 4: Create a Wine Community

In ancient Greece, wine devotees would come together to share their devotion to Dionysius, the God of the Vine. They called these events *symposiums,* which literally means "drinking together." The participants reclined in special couches spaced evenly around a room with a large bowl of wine in the center. It was both a social and spiritual event, with the night beginning with toasts to all the gods, to the heroes especially in your family, and finally to the great God Zeus. Wearing garlands of flowers and filled with wine, the conversation often turned to love, politics, and philosophy. Once adequately lubricated, they would venture into the streets for frivolous fun and sometimes more. These moments were called *komos,* which is where we get the root for comedy. The same group would meet regularly for these activities. They were called *hetaireia,* the companions. They formed tight bonds, so much so that Plato worried that loyalty to them surpassed family or state. While the conditions have changed, wine is still leading to such groups and its link to community is one of the most important parts of its role as a source of spiritual meaning for devotees.

Wine seems to want to be shared. "Is it ever alright to drink alone?" I once asked a thoughtful Italian-American winemaker who visited my class. "Of course not," he replied, "You have to drink with someone to talk to like a friend, a dog, or…a plant." While I rarely talk to my plants about what I am drinking, the impulse to share a wine is something strong. No matter how profound or transformative the interior experience might be, wine tends to be a social experience. Even wine devotees are suspicious of those who drink regularly alone.

The shared suspicion toward solo drinking often leads to the intense, tight communities among those dedicated to wine. Some tasting groups are more intimate and secretive than Opus Dei. While usually much larger, wine clubs are often designed to mimic social groups: near my university alone, there is the James Gang (Tobin James), the Black Bear Society (Zaca Mesa), the Tribe (Adelaida Cellars), the Winner's Circle (Bridlewood), Club des Amis (L'Adventure), and VINsiders (Tablas Creek). Part of the appeal of the cult wineries, as was apparent in chapter two, is the association with the group. For all these wine communities, wine is the center around which the community revolves.

Are these wine communities any different than any other shared interest group, such as a car club or a knitting club? Perhaps so. The bond within a group is largely determined by the depth of shared experience, rather than time. So a group that goes through trauma together or difficult times forms closer ties than ordinary work colleagues, even though the cumulative time together of the latter usually far exceeds the former. Wine devotees come together seeking experiences that dislodge them from normal existence, as great wines can, and then touch them in ways that literally are ineffable for the individual but occur within social environments that demand sharing. The inebriating quality of wine only facilitates the sharing of such experiences. As such, the experience of great wine in a community is one of the few deeply personal events we experience normally within a group. A spiritual experience during a religious service or a music concert might be others. These moments create what cultural anthropologist Victor Turner deemed, "Communitas": a shared and intense feeling of close connection to others. It is the electricity you feel between people as bonds form within a group and then set. It is a sudden coherence that occurs not across minds but in the instinctual, emotional, and spiritual realms. For Turner, we live for these moments when we all come together and stand outside of time and 'normal' life. In wine communities, drinking becomes a vehicle for such communitas. The need for communitas is even more significant than ever, as an examination of community demonstrates.

In the 1960s, roughly 8% of all Americans were involved in bowling leagues, making it one of the most popular group sports in America ever. Today, less than 1% are involved in bowling leagues, a drop of over 90%. People are still bowling; however, they are just bowling alone, which provides the title for one of the great books of the last decade by Harvard Sociologist Robert Putnum. It chronicles the loss of community structures in America, though the trend is similar throughout the world. By almost every measure, our participation in and our identity with our surrounding communities is more unclear now than it has ever been.

At the macro-level, our participation in our governing system as measured by voter turnout and political volunteering has declined substantially. Less people are feeling as if they have a political stake in their community. Participation in civic organizations such as Rotary and Kiwanas has fallen by nearly 90%. As average home sizes have increased dramatically and become temperature-controlled, the number of people feeling a connection to their neighbors has dropped in half in the last 50 years. Overall, we just spend less time with others: the time Americans spend informally socializing and the average number of dinner parties in the home have both dropped in half since 1965. The ease of travel and job instability has led to less time with extended families and a weakening connection to larger family groups. We find ourselves more alone and lonelier: nearly one in three people in America feel they have no one with whom to discuss important matters— this number has doubled over the past ten years.

Social Scientists have tried to quantify this overall decline by developing a metric to judge the degree of community-ness experienced by people: it is called "social capital." It is an attempt to measure the extent to which our lives are tied to other people and we feel that we belong to a community or network. While it is difficult to quantify, the general scholarly consensus is that social capital has declined by about a third in the past three decades. That is, after six or seven decades of nearly continual growth previously, America and most of the industrialized world have increasingly become social isolationists, separated from others. We feel disconnected and we are.

And worst of all, we are becoming increasingly so. The tragedy is that the degree of social capital is the single greatest predictor of the health and happiness of both the individual and society. The modern crisis is, in part, a challenge to rediscover the social cohesion that we crave but seems to be becoming more and more elusive. Online social media and virtual worlds are filling part of the gap, but people are still craving other outlets for meaningful community. This desire for community can now occur through wine groups.

Wine devotees thus gain both social capital and regular access to *communitas* through their drinking groups. They also may discover how to love others. Edouard Kressman argues that fine wine shared in a group creates the aura of "respect without which one cannot love…[and through which] learns to love other men better."[1] They discover in them part of the magic that once pervaded the symposia in ancient Greece. They may not toast to the gods at the start of the evening, but they toast to each other, their *hetaireia*, their companions. This togetherness is one of the broadest appeals to wine, and it always has been. It is one of the great pleasures in life, as wine writer Jay McInerney coyly observes: "Let's be honest: there's only one activity more satisfying than drinking good wine with good food; and if you're drinking wine in the right company, the one pleasure, more often than not, will lead to the other."[2]

Today some of the strongest of these congregations are virtual. The World Wine Web (WWW) has exploded over the last decade, with blogs and online communities creating new ways for wine devotees to join glasses. The web allows for commenting upon wine at a global level; one of the largest communities is CellarTracker.com with over 500,000 users providing 7 million wine reviews by 2017. While the major magazines such as Wine Advocate and Wine Spectator also have online forums, the most interesting are the independent ones for wine devotees such as wine berserker in the US and *La Passion du vin* (Passion for Wine) in France. *La Passion du Vin's* charter declares it as a place of "exchanges and meetings;" one of its co-founders calls the founding of the community a "story of great friendships, a sacred adventure" while another co-founder reminds the congregants that a wine does not just have flavor, but also the "stories and experiences of those who accompany" its drinking.[3]

Wine berserkers has much of the same attitude and extends the community offline as well with an annual Berserker Day festival (January 27th), up to four Berserkerfests a year in various locations, an annual ski and wine event, and other staples of communities such as people designated to welcome new members. At these events, the congregants wear name tags that prominently display their online sign, their secret symbol within the fraternity. While there are many forums on these sites, the core is the same process above: having a bottle of wine and wanting to share one's thoughts with others. This ritual is a primary mechanism in the creation of a wine congregation. It shows that it is not just sipping wine that makes a wine devotee but sipping wines with others, and talking about it afterwards.

Practical Tips for Cultivating a Wine Community

Sometimes spontaneous wine communities arise, especially when one finds kindred souls at the tail end of a particularly generous wine tasting. However, a meaningful spiritual life with wine usually requires more conscious community building. Although wine will be the elixir, one has to create the conditions for those moments of collective effervescence to arrive. The centerpiece of this project is the regular wine tastings, which are the equivalent of the communal religious gatherings in more traditionally religious environments.

Every wine tasting is an opportunity to bring the community together, reestablishing the links to each other and to wine. As with any regular service, such events need a balance of the familiar and the fresh. Much like the liturgical order of the Catholic Mass, the general framework should remain relatively consistent. Variability is offered usually by the theme of the evening. Consider creative themes for the tastings, such as:

- Same varietal across countries (e.g., cabernet around the world)
- Multiple varietals within the same country or region (e.g., Argentinian wines)
- A ladder or multiple years of the same wine (e.g., Ten consecutive years of Beckmen syrah)
- A horizontal of a given producer (e.g., all the 2005 wines of Gaja)
- Obscure grape varietals
- Wines with the worst/best labels
- Best bottle of wine from one's cellar

- Wine competitions such as French v. Napa cabernets or 2011 v. 2010 Chiantis
- Games, such as matching wines to critics descriptions or drawing competitions to create the most appropriate name and label for a wine blindly tasted

Be creative. The point of the themes is to create an environment where conversations are fostered and connections formed. Creating such bonding can be enhanced by framing the sharing part of the encounter with questions that will stimulate discussion. Instead of asking simply whether one likes/dislikes a wine or what point total you might give it, you might ask questions that draw people out, such as:

- What emotions does this wine evoke?
- What images, associations, colors, or memories does it inspire?
- What music does it bring to mind?
- If this wine was a painting, who would be the artist?
- If this wine was a celebrity, who would it be?
- If this wine was a car, what would it be?
- If this wine was an item of clothing, what would it be?

Here is the point: the secret to communal bonding is found when wine is employed as a launching pad for deeper conversations about the self and the larger world. Questions that force people to move beyond the technical judgments of wine tasting not only put people at ease (they require no expertise) but they also become indirect means of self-revelation to others. As one shares a memory or an association with the wine, inevitably one is sharing a part of oneself with the group; when everyone does this, the tenor of the event becomes deeper, more open, and more vulnerable. The wine becomes like a Rorschach test in which, as people reveal what they see, they are revealing themselves.

Certain activities can also be incorporated to enhance the likelihood of creating an environment where the bonds of community are more likely to take hold. For example, one can suggest that participants share their perception of the wines in poetic form such as haiku. Another option is to repeat some of the famous experiments in wine, such as the (in)ability of people to determine white wines from red in a blind tasting, or testing the correlation between written and musical tasting notes. Perhaps one might want to test which foods go with which wines by laying out five foods and five wines, challenging people to discover the best fit. Another option might be to have a contest to blend all the wines in the table to create the best blend. Have the tasting of each wine begin with a toast or a blessing. The point of all these exercises is to use wine as a tool to draw people out of themselves and toward each other. The intoxicating attribute of wine will eventually break down inhibitions and usually provide the levity to push the evening along, no matter how silly the activity might appear to the sober mind.

While most people on the spiritual path of wine accept the adage, "Life is too short to drink poor wine," the quality of the wine is usually not the critical element of communal bonding. In fact, some of the most memorable wine experiences can be the wines that are off in unfortunate ways; few things bind a group like micro-identification of precisely what sort of diaper smell exudes from a tainted Bordeaux, for example. Nevertheless, experiencing surprising or profound wines together often forges the unbreakable ties within a wine community.

Much like watching a strikingly beautiful sunset together or suddenly finding yourself singing in harmony a song of praise, the shared unexpected moments with wine are usually the ones that hold the most durable meaning, for you are experiencing one of the rare moments when something breaks through the din of normal existence. Sharing a wine of impossible beauty, discovering a five dollar bottle that tastes like a hundred dollar bottle, or falling in love with a newly discovered varietal can be transformative events. By their very nature, one cannot plan for these events to occur but one can create the conditions by which they are more likely to occur. A group of close wine friends is one element of such conditions; in all my interviews, I never heard of a wine epiphany occurring around enemies. Yet there is also a degree of chance or perhaps providence involved: you might consciously create a close wine community but those magical wine moments might ultimately be up to the wine gods themselves.

Becoming A Wine Devotee: Step 5: Discover Spiritual Inebriation

66"I am a bulldog running along at the feet of Jesus, barking at what He doesn't like", declared Carrie Nation, the most famous promoter of abstinence from alcohol at the turn of the century. Standing at over six feet tall, Nation bore a frightful scowl. She walked into bars, greeted the bartender with a polite enough, "Good morning, destroyer of men's soul," and then proceeded to wield her hatchet and bible, unleashing the fury of both in rapid fire. Accompanying her righteous anger was often a choir of chaste women who sang hymns in the background. Once, Jesus himself came to Nation in a vision, validating not just her ministry but also her "hatchitations," even if she was arrested dozens of times by the worldly authorities. Her biweekly newsletter, *The Smasher's Mail*, and her newspaper, *The Hatchet*, together with numerous speaking tours made her famous throughout America. While she never succeeded in banning alcohol consumption in America during her lifetime, the rise of prohibition in the 1920s represented her posthumous triumph and the antithesis to everything argued in this book.

While today people are not hatcheting wine bars with holy fury, there are still people who are uncomfortable with an alcoholic beverage playing a central role in one's religious life. For them, the premise of this book strikes them as somewhere between absurd and sacrilegious. The list of wine detractors is long: Buddhists, Mormons, Muslims, Methodists, and many others. While their arguments differ, they usually dwell on wine's intoxicating properties, which lead to clouded minds, impure souls, and become a gateway to immoral behavior. In short: wine leads to drunkenness and drunkenness leads to no good.

The presumption is that, as the Methodist church argued in 1832, "we are the more disposed to press the necessity of entire abstinence because there seems to be no safe line of distinction between the moderate and immoderate use of intoxicating drinks."[1] Indeed, for some drinkers there is no distinction between consuming wine and being a drunkard; they are called alcoholics and there is no way to justify any use of wine under these conditions. Yet, while wine can be abused, one should not assume this abuse is inevitable, and there is no reason to throw the baby out with the bathwater. There must be a middle way for the rest of us. What could a moral, responsible, and meaningful spiritual use of inebriation look like?

The Role of Alcohol in a Spiritual Relationship to Wine

At the end of the 16th century, Elizabethan writer Thomas Nashe surveyed his friends and neighbors in the evening and made the following astute observations about his fellow human's relationship to alcohol:

> *The first is ape drunk, and he leaps and sings and hollers and danceth to the heavens. The second is lion drunk, and he flings the pots about the house, calls his hostess whore, breaks the glass windows with his dagger, and is apt to quarrel with any man that speaks to him. The third is swine drunk - heavy, lumpish, and sleepy, and cries for a little more drink and a few more clothes. The fourth is sheep drunk, wise in his own conceit when he cannot bring forth a right word. The fifth is maudlin drunk, when a fellow will weep for kindness in the midst of his ale, and kiss you, saying "By God, Captain, I love thee; go thy ways, thou dost not think so often of me as I do of thee. I would, if it pleased God, I did not love thee so well as I do"- and then he puts his finger in his eye, and cries.[2]*

It appears that humans in a stupor have always been a funny bunch. We have all witnessed the manifold ways in which people unsteadily navigate the non-spiritual paths to intoxication. Inevitably, one cannot shy away from the fact that the magical mystery journey into wine is ultimately an intoxicating one. Any study of the spirituality of wine needs to address directly and honestly the role of alcohol in the spiritual journey into wine.

I have to recognize that alcohol is theoretically not necessarily required for most of the elements that make wine spiritual;

that is, one can imagine a link to place, mystery, transcendence, and community without any alcohol. However, the inebriating quality of wine plays a critical supportive role. Without the inebriating qualities of wine, I cannot imagine the possibility of seeing wine as a vehicle for spiritual growth.

On the one hand, I have come to see the role of alcohol as an intensifier of the existing conditions, sort of like the role of MSG in food. The latter does not have any flavor in itself but rather makes existing flavors in the food more pronounced. Likewise, the inebriating properties can really bring people together quickly; as we described in a previous chapter, a dinner party gets going once the wine has been poured. Alcohol seems to make mysteries more intense, transcendent experiences more uplifting, and connections to place more detectable. Like MSG, alcohol is a natural substance than can be taken to excess, but when employed appropriately, it turns the ordinary into extraordinary. It is the difference between Domaine de la Romanée-Conti and Welch's.

At some point, however, alcohol moves from being an intensifier to being a limiting force on experiences. Likes dogs in front of food, our instinct seems to be to maximize the experience to the greatest extent we can, even if it makes us throw up. However, in the mature wine devotee, the horizon of drunkenness limits the amount of wine we can drink. We may want to taste all the syrah of the Rhône Valley in a day, but we physically cannot because of the alcohol. We may want to discover insight in a full complement of a multiple flights of wines, but the prospect of drunkenness

174

limits it. We may want to spend days exploring wines with friends, but the alcohol usually puts boundaries around such duration. Thus, alcohol regulates our experiences. It gives us a taste but does not allow us to be totally satiated. This keeps us going until the last drop of the last glass of wine of our lives.

The midpoint between intensification and limitation is the sweet spot for which wine drinkers aim. It is what the Australians call getting a bit pissed and perhaps Americans call the perfect buzz. Finding such a virtuous midpoint is a learned quality and essential for an on-going relationship with wine, even if alone it is not sufficient to make wine spiritual. The spiritual path into wine requires the inability to regularly locate and settle at the midpoint between intensification and limitation. As with most meaningful endeavors, wine requires a kind of discipline, a sort of asceticism amidst the hedonistic core pursuit. Without it, wine becomes just another drink and the devotee becomes just another drunk.

Cultivating A Spiritual Drunkenness

Holy drunkenness, blessed intoxication or sanctified inebriation is not easy to speak about responsibly, since the line between spiritual and non-spiritual drunkenness is not always stark and tends to shift, especially as evenings wear on. While finding the midpoint between intensification and limitation is part of the path, it is not enough because being "moderately" inebriated can be non-edifying or carnal. In fact, although intoxication usually comes with pleasure, the journey described in this book is not primarily about physical pleasure but spiritual development. It means having a certain spiritual attitude toward the journey to inebriation. It is about cultivating a certain openness, transparency, and receptivity to wonder that is not as easy to find sober.

Perhaps it works something like this: we all have extraneous factors that shape our worldviews. These factors are often the baggage of our past and the blinders from our present. They inhibit clarity in the conscious mind for they muddle the frame so much that it is difficult to see the path of wisdom. We are usually not aware of them but even when we are, they are familiar security blankets protecting us from those parts of ourselves and the world that we wish not to confront. Drunkenness with the right attitude tends to unfurl those blankets and expose those familiar patterns upon which we rely. We become comparatively mentally naked, temporarily stripped of those extraneous factors that stymie our development. We are liberated from who we were.

In this way, holy inebriation can lead to a clearer head to see the world, not a clouded one. There may be some precedent in history for such a heretical idea. The ancient Greek historian Heroditus tells us that the Persian kings of his day would make as many decisions as possible drunk, for wisdom came with wine.[3] A bit later, German kings had a similar practice.[4] Achieving this state of clarity is tricky for undoubtedly too much wine usually leads to poor decisions, as many day-after mornings have proved, but the right amount with the right attitude crystallizes issues in ways that are difficult for most people sober.

In the end, holy inebriation allows one to see the world in a different way than we normally do.[5] It allows us to get beyond ourselves, at least as we normally encounter the world. This is why intoxication has so often been associated with artists—drugs and alcohol have been the muses of great artists from Van Gogh to Picasso. There is a famous quote about this by the French author Henri Balesta, who said about absinthe that it is the search for "an artificial paradise, removed from the bonds of reality, where the drinker's craziest, most frenzied thoughts are garbled in poetic form."[6] Balestra seems to have identified an important point: intoxication breaks down the social guards that divide people, dethrones the tyranny of the right brain, and blurs the lines between the physical and the spiritual. It allows us to get beyond the here and the now as it is commonly (if falsely) delineated.

This ability is the root of the spiritual use of intoxication: with the world as we know it partially deconstructed, we are open to the realm of mystery and wonder where the spirits dwell. Wine becomes a gateway drug to a place more profound, deeper, and more Real. Herein quite possibly lies the fruit of the soul of wine: it may be a window into the divine. But, of course, the poet Charles Baudelaire told us all that long ago:

One eve in the bottle sang the soul of wine:
"Man, unto thee, dear disinherited,
I sing a song of love and light divine —
Prisoned in glass beneath my seals of red.

Carrie Nation saw wine as inevitably a destructive force; I have tried to show that it can be a constructive one. In the end, however, it is up to each of us to choose. What do we see, *"prisoned in glass beneath my seals of red?"* Will we find the spirit in wine or something else? Only the bottom of the bottle will reveal the truth for you.

Practical Tip for Cultivating Spiritual Drunkenness: Drink Monastically

Picking up this book, many of you probably assumed that wine-drinking monks would figure prominently, yet they have not so far. In fact, the relationship between monks, who are famous for their wine and beer making, and religion is often misunderstood. Their motivation for making wine was not originally overtly spiritual.

The most enduring structure for monastic life was a walled monastery that kept the world out and the monks within to form a sort of an idealized Christian society grounded in mutual love and piety. To create this utopia removed from the devil's snares, they had to be as self-sufficient as possible. Herein lies the motivation to make wine: of course, they needed wine for communion, but their primary use was for daily drinking as part of a wider quest to be self-sufficient. Historically, people drank wine rather than water because the water was unsafe to drink. The monks were no different; it was a part of their life just as much as bread, prayer, and chastity (though perhaps a case could be made that wine worked against the latter). The most famous rule written by St. Benedict proscribes about a half liter (roughly 2/3 of a bottle) per monk per day. Today, I am accused of being a drunkard for religiously carrying out St. Benedicts monastic dictates, but for his time, it was nothing short of pious.

The records suggest that the monks may have drunk far more than their 2/3 of a bottle allotment. It is said that Abbot Adam of Angers in ninth century France drank so much wine that his skin became dyed with wine and his body became immune from corruption—a worthy life goal in my humble estimation. An old drinking song in France suggests that the monks even had a bit of competition among themselves for drinking wine. It goes: *"To drink like a Capuchin is to drink poorly, To drink like a Benedictine is to drink deeply, To drink like a Dominican is pot after pot, But to drink like a Franciscan is to drink the cellar dry!"* St. Francis, the founder of the Franciscans, would undoubtedly be proud of this victory in the monastic oenological Olympiad. However, not all were happy that the monks had such a reputation for drinking. One of the reasons that St Bernard left the Benedictines of Cluny in 1112 to start the Cistercian Order was because the former drank so much wine. It seems we can safely say that wine flowed as freely as absolution in medieval monasteries.

When these monasteries were large, as they often were in the West, their wine operations could become quite significant. Consider a monastery of 500 monks who drink the prescribed amount of 2/3 of a bottle per day, outside of fasting days. Such a monastery would have to make the equivalent of 7,000 cases of wine each year just for their own consumption.[7] Although records are scarce, this analysis is consistent with a mid-sized German monastery of the era that reported producing the equivalent to about 4,600 cases a year for their internal use.[8] Since they often made additional communion wine for use in nearby parishes and still more for outside sales, the wine operation at a typical monastery must have rivaled a medium-sized modern winery. As God's winemakers, the medieval Christian monks could have drawn inspiration from the ancient Jews: in Gibeon just north of Jerusalem, archeologists discovered a wine cellar from the seventh century BCE that stored the equivalent of 11,000 cases in 40 liter jars.[9] Such ancient precedents should reassure contemporary winemakers: they belong to *another* of the oldest professions in the world.

The monks were celebrated for the quality of the wine. The monks, especially in Burgundy, were known for literally tasting the soil and isolating the best vineyards by building walls around them, called *Clos*. Nearly a millennium later, many of these famous vineyards still produce the best wine in the world and their walls lined with crosses and other shrines built into them stand as testament to the monastic forefathers who once stopped and prayed in them while tending the vines.

The monastic wine was so good that during the period of the Avignon papacy, Pope Urban V decreed in 1364 that monasteries from Burgundy that sent their wine to rivals in Rome would be excommunicated. And when the problem between the rival popes dissipated, the pope at the time considered that perhaps it was not worth going back to Rome because it was so difficult to bring wine from Burgundy there. A legend says that the eighth century Emperor Charlemagne was such a fan of monastic wine from the region of Corton in Burgundy that his wife demanded they plant white grapes so it wouldn't stain his beard when it spilled, thus introducing to the world perhaps the finest white wine ever known, Burgundian chardonnay. As the French Renaissance writer Francois Rabelais concluded about monks and wine: "Never yet did a man of worth dislike good wine, it is a monastic truism."[10]

Yet, the lesson of the monks is not their proclivity to drink copious amounts of fine wine, but rather *how* they drunk their wine. They saw their wine as part of their spiritual development, not opposed to it. Wine became a vehicle to practice Christian virtue. For example, among Dominicans, there is a rule that at the common table, you can never pour yourself wine. Rather, the monks see wine as an opportunity to share with others. If it turns out that the wine is gone after passing around the table and there is none left for you, you have sacrificed a small part of yourself for the good of others.

As a result, wine is always seen as a gift, both in the narrow sense that it was given to you by a monastic brother but also in the wider sense of being a gift from God. In this worldview, the viticulturalist and winemakers were merely the hands of God, who guides oenological miracles into existence each day. The goal in drinking becomes not to escape the realities of this world through wine but to find God within the world of wine. Wine becomes a vehicle for divine discovery. Every glass becomes a form of communion, for God is within it. For those who drink monastically, God can indeed be found at the bottom of the glass. As Ben Franklin realized, wine becomes "a constant proof that God loves us and wants us to be happy."

One does not have to believe in a Christian God to drink monastically. It only requires an attitude of openness and gratitude when you drink. It means changing the way we approach wine. The Greek word for repentance is *metanoia*, which means literally change the orientation of your mind.

The path to seeing wine spiritually begins with *metanoia*. It means cultivating connection, mindfulness, mystery, and community as you drink. With this new mindset, the effects of alcohol do not keep you from the spiritual path but propels it. It is not drunkenness but holy inebriation and a spiritual discipline. So whatever your tradition, drink like a monk, preferably with the finest pinot.

The Sprit of Wine
Sang in my glass, and I listened
With love to his oderous music,
His flushed and magnificent song.
'I am health, I am heart, I am life!'
For I give for the asking
The fire of my father, the Sun
And the strength of my mother, the Earth.
Inspiration in essence, I am wisdom and wit to the wise,
His visible muse to the poet,
The soul of desire to the lover,
The genius of laughter to all.

William Ernest Henley, 1849-1903

Select Bibliography

Allhoff, Fritz (ed.) *Wine and Philosophy: A Symposium on Thinking and Drinking.* Maldon, MA: Blackwell Publishing, 2008.

Burnham, Douglas and. Skilleas, Ole M. *The Aesthetics of Wine.* Hoboken, NJ: Wiley-Blackwell, 2012.

Cain, Todd. *The Philosophy of Wine: A case of truth, beauty, and intoxication.* Montreal: McGill-Queen's University Press, 2011.

Coulobe, Charles A. (ed.) *The Muse in the Bottle : Great Writers on the Joys of Drinking.* New York : Citadel Press, 2002.

Ferre, Georges. *L'Âme du Vin: Symbolisme et spiritualité dans les trois religions.* Paris: Éditions Dervy, 2012.

Fuller, Robert C. *Religion and Wine: A Cultural History of Wine Drinking in the United States.* Knoxville: The University of Tennessee Press, 1996.

Harpur, Tom. *The Spirituality of Wine* Kelowna, Canada: Wood Lake Books, 2004.

Heskett, Randall and Butler, Joel. *Divine Vintage: Following the Wine Trail from Genesis to the Modern Age.* New York: Palgrave Macmillan, 2012.

Hurley, Jon. *A Matter of Taste: A History of Wine Drinking in Britain.* Stroud, Gloucestershire: Tempus Publishing, 2005.

Johnson, Hugh. *The Story of Wine.* London: Mitchell Beazley Publishers, 1989.

Kramer, Matt. *Making Sense of Wine.* Philadelphia: Running Press, 2003.

Kreglinger, Gisela H. *The Spirituality of Wine.* Grand Rapids, MI: Eerdmans, 2016.

Lukacs, Paul. *Inventing Wine: A New History of One of the World's Most Ancient Pleasures.* New York : W. W. Norton & Company, 2012.

Pitte, Jean-Robert. *Le vin et le divin.* Paris: Fayard, 2004.

Scruton, Roger. *I Drink, Therefore I am: A Philosopher's Guide to Wine.* London: Continuum, 2010.

Seward, Desmond. *Monks and Wine.* London: Mtchell Beazley Publishers, 1979.

Smith, Barry C. (ed.) *Questions of Taste: The Philosophy of Wine.* Oxford: Oxford University Press, 2007.

Theise, Terry. *Reading Between the Wines.* Berkeley: University of California Press, 2010.

Varriano, John. *Wine: A Cultural History.* London: Reaktion Books, 2011.

ABOUT THE AUTHOR

Dr. Stephen Lloyd-Moffett is a professor of Religious Studies at Cal Poly, San Luis Obispo, amateur winemaker, and caretaker of a backyard vineyard. He holds a Master of Arts and PhD in Religious Studies from University of California, Santa Barbara as well as a Master of Theology from St. Vladimir's Orthodox Theological Seminary. He is the author of *Beauty for Ashes: The Spiritual Transformation of a Modern Greek Community* (St. Vladimir's Press, 2010) and numerous articles on comparative mysticism, asceticism, community living, and early Christianity. A dynamic, popular community lecturer, he is the recipient the Cal Poly College of Liberal Arts teaching award, the President's Community Service Award, and was named one of the Top 20 Under 40 by the San Luis Obispo Tribune. He also co-founded The Lavra, a community and gathering place in Arroyo Grande, California.

Endnotes

Part I: The Spiritual Journey of Wine Devotees
Chapter 1: The Stages of Wine Devotion

[1] Kermit Lynch, *Adventures on the Wine Route: A Wine Buyer's Tour of France* (London: The Bodley Head, 1988) 226.

[2] Campbell Mattinson, *Why the French Hate Us,* (Prahran, Victoria: Hardie Grant books, 2007) 14-5

[3] Matt Kramer, *On Wine* (New York: Sterling Publishing, 2010) 30.

[4] Terry Theise, *Reading Between the Vines* (Berkeley: University of California Press, 2010) 49, 50.

[5] Len Evans, "A man of legendary charm and impeccable taste" *The Australian*1 June 2004 A:14.

[6] The story is recounted in Jon Hurley, *A Matter of Taste: A History of Wine Drinking in Britain* (Stroud, Gloucestershire: Tempus Press, 2005) 132.

[7] The angel's share is a wine term for the portion of wine in a barrel that evaporates.

Chapter 2: The Doctrines and Dogmas of the Church of Wine

[1] http://winechurch.com/

[2] A point discussed in Andrew Barr, *Wine Snobbery: An Insider's Guide to the Booze Business* (London: Faber & Faber, 1988) 144-5.

[3] While I don't purport to understand all the chemistry, those that do explain to me that wine grapes have upward of 800

separate compounds that shape the taste of wine, with oak, yeasts, and additives potentially adding many more. How can the myriad of combinations be captured in 100 distinct descriptors of the aroma wheel?

4 Andrew Jefford in *The New France*, (London: Mitchell Beazley, 2006) p. 44.

5 Andrew Jefford writes haiku as well as the following website: http://www.winehaiku.com/

6 These include Charles Spence "Wine and Music" in *The World of Fine Wine* 31 (2011) 96-103; Clark Smith, "Liquid music: resonance in wine". *Wines and vines*, 92(3), p.60.

7 Discussed in Spence, "Wine and Music" 100.

8 See W. Blake Gray, "Music to drink wine by: Vintner insists music can change wine's flavors" *San Francisco Chronicle* (Friday, November 2, 2007) Column F1. I thank Australian wine writer Max Allen for introducing me to this term and exploring together the implications of it. It is important to note that synesthesia is not using metaphors from other senses to describe wine; one is not saying the wine is *like* a minor chord to me, but rather one experiences the wine as a minor chord.

Chapter 3: The Rituals of Wine

1 Patrick McGovern describes this in his *Uncorking the Past* (Berkeley: University of California Press, 2009) 100.

2 1 Samuel 16:20.

3 See *The Art of Drinking* edited by Philippa Glanville and Sophie Lee, (London: V&A Plublications, 2007) 103. Also, Nicholas Rootes, *The Drinker's Companion* (London: Victor Gollancz, 1987) 25.

4 In Glanville and Lee, *The Art of Drinking*, 105.

5 See *Historia Regum Britanniae*, Book VI, chapter 12.

[6] Quoted in Reza Aslan, *No God but God* (New York: Random House, 2005) 214.

[7] Claude Fischler, *Du Vin* (Paris: Editions Odile Jacob, 1999) 29.

Chapter 4: The Mysticism of Wine

[1] Jancis Robinson writes that a fine wine is "capable of reaching not just your throat and your nose but your brain, your heart, and occasionally your soul, too." *Tasting Pleasures: Confessions of a Wine Lover* (London: Penguin, 1997) 24-25.

[2] This spiritual vision is behind the *Matrix* film series and bears structural similarities to Buddhism.

[3] One detects nearly an identical dynamic in one of my favorite wine descriptions, written by the Australian wine critic Philip White about a 2005 Castagna Sangiovese: "Sometimes I think she glimpses at me, over her shoulder, but not often. No white of eye, only mascara and cheekbone. She sits here on my desk with her back to me. Once, I thought I saw lipstick, but so fleeting it may have been a smudge in my brain, a tragic shard of lust. It's all shiny black leather, disappearing in the dark to a raven muss of hair. She's been eating morello cherries and Valrhona Coeur de Guanaja 80% chocolate, and she's wearing Jean Desprez Bal à Versaille to enhance the fact that she hasn't showered for days. When she moves her legs, I hear stockings. And that scarlet Louboutin clack."

[4] Meadows, *The Pearl of the Cote,* (Tarzana, CA: Burghound Books, 2010) Xiii.

[5] For a fascinating discussion of the physiological differences in taste see Francois Percival's articles in the *World of Fine Wine*, issues 32,33,34 (2011).

[6] See a summary of the research in Adrienne Lehrer, *Wine and Conversation* (Oxford: Oxford University Press, 2009) 190-191.

[7] As quoted in Evan Mitchell, Brian Mitchell, *The Psychology of Wine: Truth and Beauty by the Glass* (Santa Barbara: Greenwood Publishing Group, 2009) 59.

[8] Nigel Bruce, "Classification and hierarchy in the discourse of wine: Émile Peynaud's *The Taste of Wine* », *ASp* 23-26 (1999) 149-164.

[9] *Nature*, 1836.

[10] *Starting From Paumanok,* v 7.

Epilogue on wine in the Mystics

[1] Based on a translation from the Chinese by John Thompson as reprinted in Charles A Coulombe, *The Muse in the Mottle: Great Writers on the Joys of Drinking* (New York: Citadel Press, 2002).

[2] Ibn al-Farid, *Diwan,* trans. RA Nicholson, *Studies in Islamic Mysticism* (Cambridge: Cambridge University Press, 1921) 184-5 as quoted in Kathryn Kueny, "Sobering Intoxication: Wine in Islam" in *World of Fine Wine* 8 (2005) 90.

Chapter 5: Pinotphilia and The Religious Fanatics of the World of Wine

[1] From French wine historian Roger Dion in John Winthrop Haeger, *North American Pinot Noir* (Berkeley: UC Press, 2004) 14.

[2] http://blogs.food24.com/wholebunch/2011/05/11/ode-to-pinot-noir/, Hunter Gatherer Vintner.

[3] Clive Coates in the Preface to *The Wines of Burgundy,* (Berkeley: UC Press, 2008) xi.

[4] Jean-Anthelme Brillat-Savarin. This rhetoric has not only been one way: If it's red, French, costs too much, and tastes like the water that's left in the vase after the flowers have died and

rotted, it's probably Burgundy. Jay McInerney, *Bacchus and Me: Adventures in the Wine Cellar* (New York: Vintage Books, 2000).

[5] Jean-Robert Pitte, *Bordeaux/Burgundy: A Vintage Rivalry,* trans. by M. B. DeBevoise, (Berkeley: University of California Press, 2008) 153.

[6] Both of these examples are from Jordan Mackay *A Passion for Pinot* (Portland, OR: Carpe Diem Books, 2008) 9-10.

[7] From Sideways. Given the patience required in dealing with Pinot, the cardinal sin is to drink a Pinot too young— something we might call (I cannot resist) pinotphilia pedophilia.

[8] Eric Asimov in the forward to Jordan Mackay *A Passion for Pinot.*

[9] Quoted in in Campbell Mattinson *Why the French Hate Us: The Real Story of Australian Wine* (Prahran, Victoria: Hardie Grant Books, 2007) 288.

[10] Wine shipper Alex Gambal at World Vinifera Conference in Seattle in 1995 as quoted by Tony Aspler on his blog on July 7, 2011: http://www.tonyaspler.com/pub/articleview.asp?id=2640&s=5.

[11] Marq De Villiers, *The Heartbreak Grape: A California Winemaker's Search for the Perfect Pinot Noir* (Toronto: Harper Collins West, 1994) 25.

[12] Muscatine, Amerine & Thompson, *Book of California Wine* (Berkeley: University of California Press, 1984).

[13] Row Eleven.com; "also Persnickety and easily prone to fits of pique, pinot noir is hard to grow, hard to make into fine wine, ages erratically in the bottle, can change from ugly colt to stalwart stallion without warning (and vice versa!), and at its best is exalted as one of the greatest of all wines." In Dan Berger "Nothing Comes Easy for Pinot Noir" as preserved in

http://www.creators.com/lifestylefeatures/creators-classics/dan-berger-on-wine/nothing-comes-easy-for-pinot-noir.html

[14] Scott Wright, founder of Oregon's Scott Paul Winery in *Passion for Pinot,* 18.

[15] Kevin Harvey, owner of Rhys Vineyards quoted in http://www.princeofpinot.com/article/1180/.

[16] *Making Sense of Burgundy* (New York: William Morrow, Co, 1990).

[17] As quoted in Natalie MacLean, *Red, White, and Drunk All Over: A Wine-Soaked Journey from Grape to Glass* (New York: Bloomsbury, 2006) p. 18.

[18] Oz Clarke *New Classic Wines,* (London: Websters/Mitchell Beazley, 1991)14. Italics added.

Part II: Steps to Becoming a Wine Devotee
Step 1: Cultivate Connection to the Wine

[1] Randall Grahm in palatepress.com.

[2] As presented in the press release for Burgundy's application to UNESCO world heritage site.

[3] Michael Suster, "Senses and Place: Toward a Definition of Terroir in the Glass" in *World of Fine Wine* 18 (2007) 104. He may be drawing on a similar analogy by Andrew Jeffords in *The New France,* 18.

[4] Furthermore, a particular type of wine reminding the drinker of its place of origin is a cultural association by the drinker, not a function of terroir's influence on the form and style of the wine.

[5] Barthes, *Mythologies* (2000 edition translated by A Lavers) (Sydney: Vintage Press, 1957) 58.

---

[6] In Steve Charters, *Wine and Society: The Cultural and Social Context of a Drink* (Oxford: Elsevier/Butterworth-Heinemann, 2006) 63.

Step 2: Mindfulness and the Art of Wine Drinking

[1] In the Talmud (a compendium of Jewish stories, laws, and biblical interpretation), there is a story of Rabbi Ishmael who was known to be a bit on the stout side. He visits the home of another famous Rabbi Simeon. And typical of proper hospitality, he offers him a glass of wine. Rabbi Ishmael drank it all in one gulp. Rabbi Simeon was unhappy and said, "Do you not agree that a man who drinks a glass all in one gulp is greedy?" Rabbi Ishmael is said to have replied, "Perhaps, but your glass is small, your wine is sweet, and my stomach is broad." Apparently, it wasn't appropriate to slam wine even back then.

Step 3: Appreciate the Mystery of Wine

[1] There is a minority opinion among contemporary Jewish scholars that hold Rashi's winemaking is a myth of history or maybe just a hobby. The most prominent spokesperson for this position is found in Haym Soloveitchik, "Can Halakhic Texts Talk History?" AJS Review 3 (1978): 153-196. However, the author's wine naiveté is evident when he argues that the soil in Troyes is too poor for good wine.

[2] In his commentary on the Songs of Solomon 7:8-10.

[3] Lubavitcher Rebbe.

[4] As a side note, one has to imagine that those vines matured remarkably fast. But reasonable chronology is not the Hebrew Bible's strong point: Noah was said to be 600 at the time.

[5] Berakoth 40a, Sanhedrin 70b, Bereishit Rabbah 15:8, 19:5.

[6] The Jewish mystical text the Zohar claims that Eve squeezed the grapes, making her the first winemaker. Zohar I, 36a, 267b.

[7] Also presented in the Zohar Noah 73a.

[8] Eiruvin 65a. See also Sanhedrin 38a.

[9] R. Huna: Baba Bathra 12b.

[10] Sota 47b. This link is itself a play on words for grape cluster sound much like *ish kol bo*, one within whom is all knowledge. It also should lead to the proverbial phrase, "that person is one grape short of a cluster."

[11] Vilna Gaon, in *Safra D'Tzniusa*, 2.

[12] Berakoth 34b.

[13] Kramer, *Making Sense of Burgundy*.

[14] Jonathon Nossiter, *Liquid Memory* (New York: Farrar, Straus and Giroux, 2010) p. 15.

Step 4: Create a Wine Community

[1] Edouard Kressman, *The Wonder of Wine* (New York: Hastings House, 1968) 211.

[2] Jay McInerney, *A Hedonist in the Cellar* (New York: Vintage Press, 2007) xxiii.

[3] Jerome Perez and Denis Friedman respectively as quoted on http://www.lapassionduvin.com/html/quisommes_nous.php. Also, from the charter: "forum est par définition un lieu d'échanges et de rencontres, où le visiteur peut livrer ses impressions et ses réflexions sur des sujets liés à la dégustation et au monde du vin." http://www.lapassionduvin.com/html/lacharte.php

Step 5: Discover Spiritual Inebriation

[1] In Fuller, *Religion and Wine: A Cultural History of Wine Drinking in the United States* (Knoxville, TN: University of Tennessee Press1996) p. 82.

[2] Pierce Penilesse his *Supplication to the Divell* (1592) with modernized spelling.

[3] Herotodus, *Histories*, 1.133.

[4] Tactitus, *Germania*, 22.

[5] Robert K Siegel argues something similar in *Intoxication: The Universal Drive for Mind-Altering Substances* (Rochester, VT: Park Street Press, 1989) 217.

[6] Siegel, *Intoxication,* 110.

[7] The monks had certain advantages in the production of wine that winemakers today do not: they had access to cheap labor at harvest times, as all the monks could come out to the field when necessary. The spiritual winemakers today must rely on paid workers. The monasteries were also exempt from taxes and most local grape growers 'tithed' 10% of their finest grapes to the nearest monastery—a status that would make any contemporary winery jealous.

[8] 11,000 gallons. Seward, *Monks and Wine* (New York: Crown Publishers, 1979) p. 33.

[9] 100,000 liters. McGovern, *Ancient Wine: The Search for the Origins of Viniculture* (Princeton: Princeton University Press, 2003) p. 232.

[10] *Gargantua and Pantagruel,* Book 1, Chapter 27.

Made in the USA
Columbia, SC
22 December 2019